THE DECADES OF TWENTIETH-CENTURY AMERICA

AMERICA IN THE 1980s

MARLENE TARG BRILL

Twenty-First Century Books · Minneapolis

Twenty-First Century Books
A division of Lerner Publishing Group, Inc.
241 First Avenue North
Minneapolis, MN 55401 U.S.A.

Website address: www.lernerbooks.com

Library of Congress Cataloging-in-Publication Data

Brill, Marlene Targ.
   America in the 1980s / by Marlene Targ Brill.
      p.   cm. — (The decades of twentieth-century America)
   Includes bibliographical references and index.
   ISBN 978–0–8225–7602–0 (lib. bdg. : alk. paper)
   1. United States—History—1969—Juvenile literature. 2. United
States—Politics and government—1981–1989—Juvenile literature.
   3. United States—Social life and customs—1971—Juvenile literature.
   4. Reagan, Ronald—Juvenile literature. 5. Nineteen eighties—Juvenile
literature. I. Title.
   E876.B753 2010
   973.927—dc22   2008050116

Manufactured in the United States of America
1 2 3 4 5 6 – VI – 15 14 13 12 11 10

CONTENTS

Former president RICHARD NIXON WAVES TO THE CROWD as he boards a helicopter to take him away from Washington, D.C., on August 9, 1974. Earlier that day, he had resigned the office of president of the United States in the wake of the Watergate scandal.

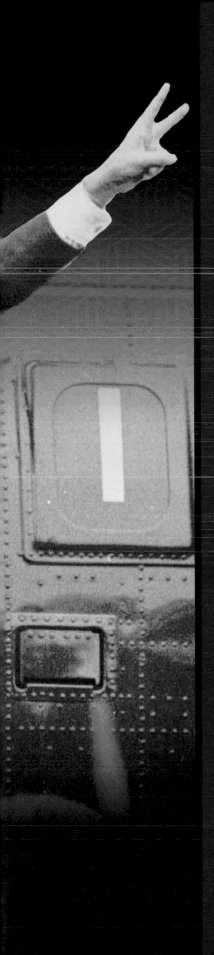

THE LASTING EFFECTS OF WAR

In 1980, as the new decade began, many wondered where the United States was headed. Critics said the country was drifting without a compass. They argued that many people focused too much on themselves and what they could buy. At the same time, the shaky economy offered low-paid workers barely enough to feed their families. Some longed for the simpler days before the riotous 1960s and 1970s when the Vietnam War (1957—1975) dominated politics, the economy, and artistic expression.

■ STOP THE WAR!

The United States had been battling Communism in Vietnam since the 1950s. Communists favor state ownership of industry, while the United States favors free enterprise and individual ownership of businesses. The United States wanted to prevent the spread of Communism in Southeast Asia. By the 1960s, the U.S. military was sending hundreds of thousands of the nation's young men to fight in Vietnam. But U.S. soldiers were dying in greater numbers as each year passed, and there seemed no end to the war. An increasing number of young people opposed the war.

5

By the early 1970s, the war was throwing the nation into chaos. Opposition to the war grew after President Richard Nixon (who served in the White House from 1968 to 1974) sent troops into the neighboring Southeast Asian nations of Cambodia and Laos. War protesters marched in the streets, took over college buildings, and disrupted government events. Some men refused to answer the draft, the required participation in the military. To show their disapproval of the war, some communities turned their backs on returning soldiers instead of hailing them as heroes, as in previous wars.

When President Richard Nixon withdrew U.S. troops from Vietnam in 1973, Americans applauded. But Nixon did not enjoy the status of a hero. By then scandal and corruption surrounded his Republican administration and eventually cost him the presidency. His reelection campaign, and even the Central Intelligence Agency (CIA), had become involved in bribery, stealing documents from the Democratic Party and planting illegal wiretaps to listen in on phone conversations. President Gerald Ford (who was in office from 1974 to 1976), Nixon's vice president and a respected longtime representative from Michigan, tried to restore confidence in government. By then, however, many citizens no longer trusted their representatives in Washington.

■ DEALING WITH POSTWAR TRAUMAS

Some citizens had hoped that when the United States ended its involvement in the Vietnam War, the country would regain its footing. Protesters in bell-bottoms and miniskirts would leave the streets. Young people and minorities would stop pressing their demands for equal rights. Funk, disco, hard rock, and protest songs would make way for an age of quieter tunes with less angry lyrics.

The nation, however, showed no signs of returning to the calm, optimism, and prosperity of earlier times. The economy was in bad shape. Waging a war in Vietnam had been expensive, and President Richard Nixon had not raised taxes to pay for it. Morale was poor. For the first time in recent history, the United States had failed as a world power.

Family trends begun in the 1960s continued throughout the 1970s. For some, traditional institutions such as

The nation, however, showed no signs of returning to the quiet, calm, optimism, and prosperity of earlier times.

marriage and children became less important than in earlier decades. More couples divorced. More single parents with children ran households. Unmarried couples lived together with little thought of marriage.

Movements that had gained traction in the 1960s and early 1970s continued. The women's movement went on pressing for equal access to jobs, pay, and birth control for women. African Americans called for the same rights as whites to vote, work, find good housing, and send their children to decent schools. Homosexuals wanted legal protection against discrimination. And individuals with disabilities came out of the shadows to push for better physical access to buildings, transportation, recreation, and jobs.

The arts—music, painting, and literature—reflected the upheaval in the nation during and after the war. Some artists produced nontraditional, abstract works that searched for meaning in a society trying to find its way. Others used their talents to make up for past inequalities by featuring women, blacks, and people with disabilities in their art. As the decade progressed, hard rock music got harder. New forms of music, such as disco, punk, funk, and new wave, appeared. The edginess of the sixties continued throughout the 1970s.

■ PEANUT FARMER GOVERNOR TO THE RESCUE

In the 1976 presidential campaign, former Georgia governor Jimmy Carter, a Democrat, promised to calm the nation by doing business differently. He had been a peanut farmer before

WOMEN RALLY FOR PASSAGE OF THE EQUAL RIGHTS AMENDMENT TO THE U.S. CONSTITUTION in Boston, Massachusetts, in 1981. Equal rights for women was a hot-button issue in the United States throughout the decade.

entering politics, and he spoke with a plain, folksy style and strong moral conviction. In campaign speeches, he pledged "never to lie to the American people." Ordinary citizens connected with his honesty and straightforward-ness. They thought he could provide the change they sought and give the nation a much-needed boost. Carter was a Washington outsider, which voters welcomed. They elected Jimmy Carter as the nation's thirty-ninth president in 1976.

Carter's administration floundered from the beginning. He achieved some successes, such as the 1978 Camp David Accords, which led to a peace treaty between Egypt and Israel. But Carter remained an outsider in his dealings with Congress, and this kept him from negotiating effectively with members of Congress. As a result, Congress refused to approve many of his programs. At the same time, events around the world compro-mised his ability to follow through on several campaign promises. His plans for welfare reform, government reor-ganization, and creation of a workable energy policy lagged.

By 1980 oil shortages had created the highest rate of inflation—the greatest rise in prices for all goods—in thirty-three years. On average, prices were rising 13 percent a year. Unemployment was soaring too. The value of the dollar in foreign coun-tries, meanwhile, had fallen. The public lost confidence in President Carter. Critics publicized his small-est failures. TV newscaster Mike Wallace later called Carter the "Fly-paper President." The media seemed to blame him for every problem the nation experienced, and the blame stuck like flies stick to flypaper.

PRESIDENT JIMMY CARTER kneels in a peanut field at his family's farm in Georgia in 1976. Carter went from peanut farmer to governor of Georgia to president of the United States.

■ BAD LUCK PRESIDENT

Of all Carter's problems, the worst occurred after Iranians ousted their former dictator, Muhammad Reza Pahlavi, early in 1979. In his place, they installed a government based on the religion of Islam. In November 1979, Iranian students in Tehran, Iran's capital, seized sixty-six American hostages. Iranians continued to hold fifty-two of the hostages for more than a year. Iranians resented the United States for supporting the shah and granting him permission to enter the United States for cancer treatment after he had been deposed.

Carter made several attempts to negotiate for the release of the hostages with the Islamic cleric Ayatollah Ruholla Khomeini, who ruled Iran. When these went unanswered, the president ordered U.S. military troops in helicopters to carry out a rescue mission. But all efforts failed, and eight servicemen died trying to reach the hostages. Carter's failure to bring the hostages home opened him to more criticism. Thereafter, he became known as the Bad Luck President. Discouraged Americans wanted to feel hopeful about their nation's future, and they longed for more faith in their leaders. When the 1980 elections rolled around, voters were ready for change.

THE WRECKAGE OF A U.S. HELICOPTER lies in the desert after failing in an attempt in April 1980 to rescue U.S. hostages held in Iran.

Former California governor RONALD REAGAN CAMPAIGNS FOR PRESIDENT in Nebraska in 1980. Reagan, the Republican nominee, ran against Democratic candidate President Jimmy Carter that year.

"**For those who have abandoned hope, we'll restore hope, and we'll welcome them into a great national crusade to make America great again! . . . The time is now . . . to recapture our destiny, to take it into our own hands.**"

—*Ronald Reagan, accepting the Republican Party nomination for president, 1980*

CHAPTER ONE

HOLLYWOOD COMES TO WASHINGTON:
RONALD REAGAN IN THE WHITE HOUSE

In 1980 the United States faced high inflation, a hostage crisis, and a sitting president with a low approval rating. This situation gave Ronald Reagan the perfect opportunity to enter the race for president on the Republican ticket against President Jimmy Carter. Reagan, a former movie actor, swept onto the national political stage with his message of hope. He believed that Americans were among the best people on Earth. He said they needed a strong leader like himself to restore national pride. Reagan's agenda focused on reducing the burden of taxes, so businesses and families could flourish. And he wanted to reduce the size of government. As he campaigned, Reagan emphasized lessening government's role in citizens' lives. He often said, "Government isn't the answer. It's the problem."

In foreign policy, Reagan promised to mend the nation's battered image overseas by sounding strong and increasing U.S. military strength. His speeches challenged Americans to dream of better, more heroic times to come. His messages were simple: reduce government spending, cut the size of the government, slash taxes by 30 percent, and never back down from enemies. Reagan appealed to a public starved for tough, unwavering leadership.

■ THE 1980 ELECTION

Ronald Reagan ran a campaign promoting "an era of national renewal," beginning with lower taxes and a smaller government. He also embraced the Republican Party platform (statement of beliefs). The party promoted prayer in public schools and public funds for religious schools. Democrats believed both were forbidden by the Constitution. Republicans also hoped to end a woman's legal right to have an abortion, even though the Supreme Court had upheld this right in the 1973 *Roe v. Wade* court case.

On November 4, 1980, Reagan defeated President Carter. George H. W. Bush became vice president. Reagan won 52 percent of the popular vote compared with Carter's 41.6 percent. John Anderson, who ran for president as an independent, won 6.4 percent. Many voters reported afterward that they voted *against* Carter and not *for* Reagan. Still, a number of southern Democrats and an overwhelming percentage of Republicans felt Reagan's conservative agenda reflected their beliefs. They greeted his win as nothing short of a revolution.

RONALD REAGAN IS SWORN IN AS THE FORTIETH PRESIDENT OF THE UNITED STATES in January 1981. His wife, Nancy Reagan, holds the Bible, as Chief Justice Warren E. Burger administers the oath of office.

FAMILY AND FRIENDS GREET FREED U.S. CITIZENS WHO HAD BEEN HELD HOSTAGE IN IRAN FOR 444 DAYS. The hostages were released on January 20, 1981—the day Ronald Reagan was inaugurated. They returned to the United States two days later.

■ THE REAGAN REVOLUTION BEGINS

On January 20, 1981, Ronald Reagan was sworn in as the nation's fortieth president. He was almost seventy years old, the oldest American to assume the office. "We must act today in order to preserve tomorrow," Reagan told the nation in his inaugural address.

A few hours after the speech, Iran released the fifty-two American hostages. Carter had been in negotiations with the Iranian government for the hostages' release. The timing of the release denied Carter the one success he most craved—the safe return of the hostages.

Reagan's election, while perhaps not a revolution, signaled change in how the nation did business. After Carter had become president, he and his family had walked up Pennsylvania Avenue from the Capitol to the White House. Evening festivities involved a casual "People's Inaugural," where peanuts and pretzels were served instead of fancy food to save money. The Reagan era, on the other hand, began with an eleven-million-dollar inaugural celebration in Washington, the most expensive in U.S. history. Reagan and his wife, former actress Nancy Davis, road in their limo to the White House. They danced through ten formal inaugural balls, many paid for by corporate and private gifts. The large number of elaborate gatherings and the many guests from the entertainment industry prompted some observers to exclaim that Hollywood had arrived in Washington.

RONALD REAGAN PLAYED GEORGE GIPP

in the 1940 film *Knute Rockne All American*. It led to his nickname the Gipper.

Ronald Reagan (1911–2004) seemed an unlikely candidate for president. He was born and raised in central Illinois, where his father was a shoe salesman who drank too much and switched jobs often. Reagan's mother worked at odd jobs when her husband was unemployed and money was tight.

Reagan played football and acted in plays at Eureka College, a small school in Illinois run by a religious group called the Disciples of Christ. After college his good looks and easygoing personality helped him break into radio and then Hollywood movies. He acted mainly in second-rate cowboy and war movies. His role as dying Notre Dame football player George Gipp in *Knute Rockne All American* (1940) earned him the nickname the Gipper. Reagan wasn't known as a great thinker. But his beliefs ran deep, and he wasn't afraid to share them.

In Hollywood, Reagan joined the actors union, the Screen Actors Guild. As its president for five years, he met people who seemed to approve of the U.S. Communist Party. Reagan feared that Communists would spread their beliefs throughout the country and change the American way of life.

When his movie career waned, Reagan turned to television. He hosted the drama series *General Electric Theater* from 1954 until 1962. As part of his job, he toured General Electric plants and spoke to employees. Reagan was an effective speaker.

In 1966 Reagan launched a successful bid to become the governor of California. During eight years as governor, Reagan fine-tuned his policies of reducing government spending and taxes. In 1968 and 1975, he tried to become the Republican nominee for president of the United States and lost each time. But his popularity as a hard-line conservative grew, until he finally won the Republican nomination and then the presidential election in 1980.

After serving as president of the United States for two terms, Reagan left office in 1989. In 1994 he disclosed he had Alzheimer's disease, a brain disease. He died a decade later, in 2004.

14

AMERICA IN THE

1980s

■ THE PRESIDENT IS SHOT

On March 30, 1981, a little more than two months into his presidency, Ronald Reagan was shot. As the president left Washington's Hilton Hotel after giving a speech, a lone gunman sprayed the crowd with bullets. One bullet pierced Reagan's side. Secret Service guards threw the stunned president into his limo and ordered the driver to the hospital.

Throughout his ordeal, the good-natured president kept jokes coming. When Reagan learned he needed surgery, he said to the doctor, "I hope you're a Republican." With a breathing tube in his airway, the former actor scribbled a note that read, "I'd like to do this scene again—starting at the hotel."

Besides Reagan, his press secretary, James Brady, Secret Service agent Tim McCarthy, and policeman Tom Delehanty were injured. Amazingly, all survived. Only Brady's injury resulted in lasting damage. Meanwhile, Reagan's astonishing recovery and the grace he showed raised his hero status with the public.

The police caught the shooter, John Hinckley Jr., immediately. Hinckley was mentally unstable and had been stalking the actress Jodie Foster. He wanted to get her attention by shooting somebody important. A jury found Hinckley not guilty by reason of insanity and committed him to a mental institution. His actions launched heated debates about gun control.

Police and Secret Service agents react after **JOHN HINCKLEY JR. SHOOTS PRESIDENT RONALD REAGAN** in front of the Hilton Hotel in Washington, D.C., on March 30, 1981.

> **"I wanted to go to the negotiating table and end the madness."**

—Ronald Reagan, in his autobiography, on the arms race with the Soviet Union, 1990

■ MILITARY MADNESS

The assassination attempt barely slowed Reagan or his plans to alter policies at home and abroad. The president hoped to change the nation's direction based on his belief that a strong image abroad depended upon military strength at home. But he found the U.S. military in sad shape because of the low number of new recruits, outdated equipment, and poor soldier morale. Reagan feared the state of the military placed the United States at a disadvantage with the Soviet Union.

Since World War II (1939–1945), the United States and its allies in Western Europe had frosty diplomatic relations with the Soviet Union and its allies. The Soviet Union was a vast country that consisted of fifteen republics. It spread from the Baltic Sea and the Black Sea in the west, all the way to the Pacific Ocean in the east. The capital was Moscow, in the Russian republic.

The Soviets based their government on the principles of Communism. After World War II, the United States feared that the Soviet Union would dominate Eastern Europe and spread Communism to Western Europe. The Soviet Union did, in fact, want to see Communism spread throughout the world. The Cold War (1945—1991) was a conflict over ideas, which threatened to become a real war. Each nation amassed weapons in an unofficial arms race, although they never used them. By the time Reagan came into office, both superpowers maintained nuclear weapons capable of destroying the world and everything in it.

"I wanted to go to the negotiating table and end the madness . . ." Reagan wrote in his autobiography, "but to do that, I knew America first had to upgrade its military capabilities so that we would be able to negotiate with the Soviets from a position of *strength*, not weakness.

To build up the U.S. military's defense against the Soviets, Reagan ordered production of a neutron bomb. This weapon would destroy its targets with radiation. Reagan further announced plans to build one hundred B-1 bombers and one hundred MX land-based missiles pointed toward Soviet targets. Reagan called these new weapons

Demonstrators march in the streets of New York City in 1982 to protest the **ARMS RACE.**

peacekeepers. He also planned to store nuclear missiles at U.S. military bases throughout Western Europe.

Peace groups protested the buildup. Marches and peace camp settlements appeared near U.S. military and nuclear sites. In one case, three thousand women camped near Seneca Falls, New York, near an army depot. These peace activists felt a strong desire to make the world a safer place to live. Reagan countered that the missiles were bargaining chips that would force the Soviets to reduce their own missile program.

In 1983 Reagan suggested his most controversial military proposal, the creation of the Strategic Defense Initiative (SDI). He hoped to commit $1.5 trillion to build a defense system that would destroy Soviet missiles from space before they reached their U.S. targets. News of the SDI program surprised even Reagan's inner circle. Some believed that the fanciful idea stemmed from the former actor's role as Secret Service agent Bass Bancroft in the 1940 film *Murder in the Air*. In the movie, Reagan's character guarded a space-age death ray similar to the proposed missile defense system. Critics charged that Reagan increasingly seemed unable to distinguish between fantasy and reality. They immediately dubbed the new program Star Wars, after the 1977 science fiction movie by George Lucas.

Reagan's calls for building up the nation's military may have escalated the pace of the arms race. The Soviets launched a costly program of military research and construction to compete with the United States. Reagan justified the expense and potential danger of the new weapons by portraying the Soviet Union as an evil empire that would do anything to spread Communism. He raised Cold War fears to heights not seen since the 1950s.

PRESIDENT REAGAN UNVEILS HIS STRATEGIC DEFENSE INITIATIVE to the nation in 1983. Reagan hoped SDI would make nuclear weapons obsolete.

AMERICA IN THE

CONTRA SPECIAL FORCES COMMANDOS train in 1985. The U.S.-supported contras worked secretly to overthrow the Sandinista government in Nicaragua.

■ BATTLES IN CENTRAL AMERICA

One of Reagan's biggest fears was that Communists would gain control of governments close to the United States. Before Reagan took office, a union of Communist-leaning groups known as the Sandinista National Liberation Front had overthrown the government in Nicaragua. By 1981 the Sandinista government had strengthened its ties with Cuba, a Communist nation in the Caribbean Sea and an ally of the Soviet Union. Reagan felt he had no other option but to become involved in Central America. He ordered support for independent fighters who could remove the left-wing government in Nicaragua.

The fighters, known as contras, were trained by the U.S. military in secret camps in the swamps of Florida. Another U.S.-backed contra group formed in Costa Rica, Nicaragua's neighbor. The Central Intelligence Agency helped contras conduct raids inside Nicaragua, and the U.S. government provided millions of dollars to aid their battles. Throughout these operations, Reagan continued to remind the public that Communists could take over Central America. He warned, "Our credibility would collapse, our alliances would crumble, and the safety of our homeland would be jeopardized" should Communists set up governments close to the United States.

■ LESSONS IN THE MIDDLE EAST

During the early 1980s, Lebanon—a small nation in the Middle East—exploded into civil war. Christians and Muslims, who practice the religion of Islam, fought for control of their country. On August 25, 1982, eight hundred U.S. Marine troops arrived in Beirut, Lebanon, as peacekeepers, along with troops from Italy and France. At first, the Lebanese greeted the Western armies as heroes. As the different factions squabbled, however, Muslims saw the United States as siding with the Christian government. Some Muslims thought the United States was an enemy of Islam.

On October 23, 1983, a truck rigged with explosives blasted through the marines' headquarters in Beirut, killing 241 marines. At first, Reagan refused to bring the marines home, despite the urging of his secretary of defense, Caspar Weinberger. Reagan finally ordered them home in January.

■ INVADING GRENADA

Two days after the massacre of U.S. Marines in Lebanon, the United States made its boldest move into Central America. On October 25, 1983, U.S. forces invaded Grenada, a 131-square-mile (339-square-kilometer) island of 110,000 people in the Caribbean Sea. The tiny nation had recently experienced turmoil when its leader was assassinated. Reagan feared the Communist government of Cuba might use the island as a staging area to give military support to Nicaragua's Sandinista government in its fight against the U.S.-backed contra forces. President Reagan used the presence of an American medical school in Grenada as an excuse to invade the island. He told the public that chaos threatened the school's six hundred American students.

U.S. MARINES PULL SURVIVORS FROM THE RUBBLE after a truck bomb exploded at marine headquarters in Beirut, Lebanon, in October 1983.

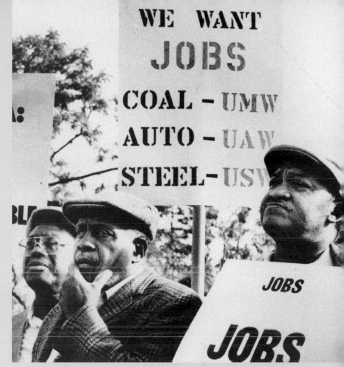

Almost two thousand marines and paratroopers stormed into Grenada. They easily overtook the island and established a temporary government. Within days, Reagan reported that the United States had restored "order and democracy." More than seven hundred Americans, many of them medical students, left the island.

The United Nations Security Council condemned the invasion by a vote of 11 to 1. But the dissenting vote, which came from the United States, was enough to kill the resolution. Nonetheless, the world took notice of the United States' aggressive president. At home some saw the invasion of Grenada as a way to divert the public's attention from the administration's failures in the Middle East. Others, however, hailed Reagan for his decision-making skills and for saving the Caribbean island from Communism.

■ THE FEEL-GOOD PRESIDENT RETURNS

In 1984, at the age of seventy-three, Reagan campaigned for a second term as president. He charmed the media and connected with everyday people with his simple, optimistic messages.

The nation's economy was emerging from a deep recession. In 1982 nine million Americans had been out of work. By 1984 the economy was improving. Reagan's cheery messages made many voters believe their country was headed in the right direction.

A few reporters, however, nicknamed Reagan the Celluloid President. (At the time, films were made of celluloid and were fed into projectors at movie theaters.) They believed his talents came from handlers, much like those who had directed his movies. Before the 1984 election, the conservative *Chicago Tribune* printed: "Mr. Reagan's . . . air-headed rhetoric on the issues of foreign policy and arms control have reached the limit of tolerance and have become an embarrassment to the U.S. and a danger to world peace." Still, the paper went on to endorse Reagan for president.

21

Reagan's Democratic opponent was Walter Mondale, a former U.S. senator from Minnesota and vice president under Carter. Mondale faced an uphill battle from the beginning. He promised to raise taxes to repay the government's debts. It was not a popular position.

Mondale selected Geraldine Ferraro, U.S. representative from New York, as his running mate. For a while, being the first to place a woman on a national ticket energized the campaign. After newspapers exposed possible financial scandals involving Ferraro's husband, however, her star value dimmed.

Then fifty-six-year-old Mondale seized on Reagan's age as an issue. But Reagan shot back, "I am not going to exploit for political purposes my opponent's youth and inexperience." His clever response effectively eliminated age from the race.

At the age of seventy-three, Reagan won a second term as president with 59 percent of the vote and leading numbers in every state except Minnesota, Mondale's home state. "The magic of opportunity—unreserved, unfailing, unrestrained—isn't this the calling that unites us?" the president said during his 1986 State of the Union address.

WALTER MONDALE AND GERALDINE FERRARO, Democratic presidential and vice-presidential nominees, respectively, in 1984, wave to the crowd at the Democratic National Convention in July of that year.

I n 1981 Justice Potter Stewart retired, leaving a vacancy on the U.S. Supreme Court. Mindful of a campaign pledge to elevate women in government, Ronald Reagan searched for a woman to fill the vacancy. He nominated Sandra Day O'Connor, a midlevel state court judge from Arizona known for being tough, fair, and Republican. Reagan hoped she shared his conservative views.

O'Connor (born in 1930) was a skillful lawyer who liked to emphasize her upbringing on a ranch near Phoenix and her role as the mother of three sons. She had passed Arizona's bar exam at a time when most women found doors closed to them at top law firms. She started her own law firm. While raising her sons, she worked part-time for the Arizona attorney general's office. This job led to her appointment as state senator in 1969 to fill a vacant seat. She managed to win an election and keep her seat. In 1973 O'Connor became the first woman majority leader of any state senate. The next year, she served as a judge in the Maricopa County Superior Court. In 1979 O'Connor was elected to the Arizona Court of Appeals.

On the Supreme Court, O'Connor often voted with the more conservative justices. But she also established herself as a key swing voter. Sometimes she cast the tie-breaking vote (in a 5 to 4 decision) to side with the more liberal justices on issues such as abortion and sexual harassment.

SUPREME COURT JUSTICE SANDRA DAY O'CONNOR was the first woman to serve on the United States' highest court.

The first female Supreme Court justice credited the women's rights movement, which pushed for equality for women, for her rise to the highest court in the nation. "The important fact about my appointment is not that I will decide cases as a woman," she said, "but that I am a woman who will get to decide cases."

O'Connor retired from the Supreme Court in 2006 to care for her husband, who was ill with Alzheimer's. She has become an advocate for research to find a cure for Alzheimer's disease. In 2009 she created the website Our Courts: 21st Century Civics (www.ourcourts.org) to help middle-school kids learn about government and have fun while doing so.

OLIVER NORTH, lieutenant colonel of the U.S. Marines, is sworn in before the House of Representatives and Senate Foreign Affairs Committee in Washington, D.C., in July 1987. North testified about his involvement in the Iran-contra affair.

CHAPTER TWO

REAGAN TAKES HIS SHOW ABROAD

POLITICS AWAY FROM HOME

During Ronald Reagan's second term, relations between the United States and the Soviet Union improved greatly. All was not well in the Middle East, however. Between 1984 and 1985, Islamic terrorists stepped up attacks on U.S. interests in the region. More than two hundred hijackings, shootings, and kidnappings occurred. Reagan believed that most plans for the attacks originated in Iran, Libya, and Lebanon, and he proclaimed their involvement often. In 1985 Reagan held Iran responsible for radical Islamic terrorists who were holding seven U.S. hostages in Lebanon, including an employee of the Central Intelligence Agency.

■ IRAN-CONTRA AFFAIR

In November 1985, the Reagan administration approved the secret sale of arms to Iran in exchange for Iran's help in freeing the seven hostages. To cover up the deal, the arms were sold to Iran through Israel. An assistant at the National Security Council, Oliver North, lieutenant colonel of the U.S. Marines, managed the exchange.

North was an enthusiastic fighter against Communism, a Vietnam veteran, and a planner of the 1983 attack on Grenada. North secretly arranged to use some of the money from the arms sale to support the contra rebels' efforts to overthrow the San-dinista government in Nicaragua. Both selling arms to Iran without congres-sional approval and secretly sending money to Nicaragua were illegal. The operation was supported and directed by high-ranking government leaders, including CIA director William Casey; his national security adviser, Robert McFarlane; and Rear Admiral John Poindexter, who became national security adviser when McFarlane left that position.

The deal never worked. Iranians gained the arms they wanted, but the ter-rorists released only three of the original seven hostages. Within a short time after the exchange, Islamic extremists seized three more American hostages.

News of the arms-for-hostages plot came to light in November 1986, expos-ing a trail of secrets and lies. At first, Reagan claimed the arms were sold to Iran to improve relations with Iranians, not to secure the release of hostages. Investigators eventually found evidence that contradicted Reagan. On Novem-ber 25, 1986, the administration admitted that it secretly sold arms to Iran in violation of the law. "This hurt Reagan in two ways," wrote reporter Kenneth Walsh. "He had promised never to negotiate with terrorists, and the diversion

PRESIDENT RONALD REAGAN AND VICE PRESIDENT GEORGE H. W. BUSH *(SITTING ON DESK, CENTER)* POSE FOR A PHOTO WITH REAGAN'S CABINET (ADVISERS). CIA director William Casey *(far right, standing)* and Defense secretary Caspar Weinberger *(far right, sitting)* were implicated in the Iran-contra affair.

of funds violated the Boland Amendment banning military aid to the contras. His credibility was in tatters."

Reagan appointed a commission, headed by a former Republican senator, John Tower, to look into the entire episode. The Tower Commission's report pointed to Secretary of State George Shultz and Defense secretary Caspar Weinberger as ringleaders. The report came down hard on the White House, asserting that Reagan was out of touch with his own administration. Journalist R. W. Apple Jr. wrote of the report: "This portrait is of a man confused, distracted, so remote that he failed utterly to control the implementation of his vision . . . [to] free American hostages and reestablish American influence in Iran."

A special prosecutor, Lawrence Walsh, conducted a legal investigation into the affair. In May 1989, a jury convicted North on three criminal counts and fined him $150,000. By then George H. W. Bush was president of the United States. Under oath in court, North testified that he had been ordered to keep silent. He added that George H. W. Bush had acted as go-between with the contras. Although the questioning uncovered participation at the highest levels of government, none of the men involved went to prison.

GEORGE SHULTZ, U.S. SECRETARY OF STATE from 1982 to 1989, was involved as a ringleader in the Iran-contra affair.

" Between Reagan, intent on something upbeat, and Gorbachev [head of state of the Soviet Union], intent on somehow ameliorating [ending] the Cold War, we had what you might call a meeting of minds, and the beginning of nuclear disarmament, even if only the beginning."

—*Isaac Asimov, author, 1989*

■ THAWING THE COLD WAR

Reagan's greatest achievement was the transformation of U.S. relations with the Soviet Union. During his first years as president, Reagan had taunted Soviet leaders with bravado about U.S. military buildups. He also criticized the leaders for violating the rights of their citizens, who went to jail if they spoke out against the government. In addition, Reagan had tried to limit Soviet influence and isolate Soviet nations internationally. He encouraged other nations not to do business with the Soviets. In one of his boldest moves to limit Soviet influence, Reagan sold China, a Soviet enemy, sensitive military technology.

On the home front, the Soviets suffered a rash of internal crises. During the first four years of Reagan's presidency, Soviet citizens witnessed three of their elderly leaders die in office. In addition, the Soviet Union's arms race with the United States drained its weak economy. Living standards declined as Soviets poured money and technology into a first-rate military with almost four million troops and about twenty-five thousand nuclear weapons.

In 1985 winds of reform blew through the Soviet Union's leadership. Fifty-four-year-old Mikhail Gorbachev became the new Soviet leader. Gorbachev believed in Communism, but he thought people needed more individual freedom. And he thought the government was too corrupt. He proposed a program of government restructuring that called for greater democracy and glasnost, or openness. "Everything pertaining to the economy, culture, democracy—all spheres—had to be reappraised, including the erosion . . . of moral values," he wrote later of his plan.

With glasnost, Soviets experienced more freedom. Citizens felt more comfortable speaking publicly for and against the government without fear of arrest. Artists expressed themselves without being censored. Newspapers printed articles critical of the government. Before Gorbachev's reforms, the government controlled all businesses and the nation's wealth. After the reforms, independent businesses opened and kept much of their profits.

Reagan saw an opening for communication and invited Gorbachev to meet with him. In an exchange of letters, both men offered to take steps toward lessening the threat of nuclear war and improving relations. On November 19 and 20, 1985, President Reagan and Gorbachev met in Geneva, Switzerland. The two leaders exchanged ideas without much progress. But they agreed to meet again in 1986, a major step forward.

Reagan and Gorbachev met again from October 10 to 12, 1986, in Reykjavik, Iceland. For almost ten hours, they discussed how they might stop their arms race. A year later, the two leaders agreed on a treaty to cut their nuclear forces in half. Both realized the future well-being of their nations depended upon reducing arms threats. "No one could win a nuclear war—and as I had told Gorbachev . . . one must never be fought," Reagan wrote.

On December 8, 1987, Mikhail Gorbachev attended his first meeting in Washington, D.C., with President Reagan. The two leaders signed the historic

PRESIDENT RONALD REAGAN *(LEFT)* MEETS WITH MIKHAIL GORBACHEV, the leader of the Soviet Union, in Geneva, Switzerland, in November 1985. They discussed ending the arms race.

Intermediate-Range Nuclear Forces Treaty (INF). The agreement required that within three years the United States would destroy 859 midrange missiles and the Soviets would destroy 3,400. After the meeting, Gorbachev met with human rights advocates and greeted bystanders.

In June 1988, Reagan visited Moscow and took the city by storm. He ventured into a Arbat shopping mall and talked with Soviet human rights groups. Each leader charmed the other's citizens and media. They shared a real friendship, and the forty-five-year conflict between the two nations subsided. When a Soviet reporter asked Reagan if the Soviet Union was still an "evil empire," Reagan replied, "No, I was talking about another time, another era."

■ THE POPULAR GIPPER

The glow from Reagan's success in dealing with Gorbachev lasted until the close of Reagan's presidency. He also received some of the credit for U.S. recovery from a deep recession. Reagan left office with an unprecedented 63 percent approval rating, topping any president in the previous fifty years. Gallup polls continually listed him as one of the "most admired men in America."

Failures and scandals could not tarnish Reagan's sunny charm and cowboy image.

The public mostly overlooked the widening gap between the nation's rich and poor and did not hold Reagan responsible for the Iran-contra affair. His popularity was unharmed by the failure of the expensive Star Wars program. Failures and scandal could not tarnish Reagan's sunny charm and cowboy image.

Reagan summarized his presidency this way: "I came here with a belief that this country, the people, were kind of hungering for a, call it a spiritual revival. . . . And I came here with plans and set out to implement them. No, we didn't get everything we asked for, but you don't fall back in defeat."

■ THE ARISTOCRAT PRESIDENT

Republican George Herbert Walker Bush hoped Reagan's light would shine on his run for president in 1988. The son of Connecticut senator Prescott Bush, he came to the campaign with a fortune from his family and the business he built drilling Texas oil. And he brought deep experience in foreign affairs. Bush was vice president under Ronald Reagan for eight years.

J esse Jackson Sr. ran in the Democratic primary elections in 1984 and 1988, each time hoping to become the party's candidate for president. Born in Greensville, South Carolina, in 1941, Jackson was a leader in the civil rights movement, which called for basic civil rights for African Americans. In the early 1960s, he helped organize sit-ins in Greensboro, North Carolina. There, African Americans sat down at whites-only restaurants to protest racial discrimination. Jackson also worked with the civil rights leader Martin Luther King Jr. until King's assassination in 1968. Jackson became an ordained minister after King died. He used his commanding speaking skills to form the Chicago-based Operation PUSH (People United to Save Humanity) to work for social justice.

During the 1980s, Jackson broadened his focus. He visited South Africa and the Middle East, trying to influence U.S. foreign policy in these regions. *Ebony* magazine called Jackson "the most charismatic, most combative, most visible black leader in America."

During the 1984 and 1988 presidential elections, he registered hundreds of thousands of southern blacks to vote. He also spoke for all poor and minorities who suffered under Reagan policies. His two campaigns were backed by his "Rainbow

JESSE JACKSON SR. speaks at the Democratic National Convention in 1988.

Coalition" of supporters who were black, Latino, women, and members of other marginalized groups.

Jackson's Rainbow Coalition did not win Jackson a presidential nomination. But his ability to persuade minorities to vote caught the attention of the Democratic Party's leaders. They asked Jackson to speak at the 1988 Democratic National Convention, which launched Michael Dukakis as the party's candidate for president.

Since then, Jackson has acted as an advocate for African Americans and for all poor people. He has continued to support bringing businesses to black communities. He also tries to help labor unions and supports the creation of more housing for the poor.

Before that, Bush had served as U.S. representative to the United Nations (1971–1972), Republican National Party chair (1973–1974), ambassador to China (1974–1975), and CIA director (1976–1977). Conservative Republican lawmakers saw him as their best hope to keep loyal Reagan supporters united. Republicans nominated Bush as their candidate for the next president.

Bush's Democratic opponent was the Massachusetts governor, Michael Dukakis. A humorless man, Dukakis had gained a reputation for being smart, honest, and businesslike. For a time, Dukakis led in the polls. But he had little experience on the international level. This put him at a disadvantage against Bush.

In his campaign, Bush talked of a "kinder, gentler nation," but his staff ran a mean-spirited campaign. They painted Dukakis as unpatriotic and soft on crime. For example, the Bush team created TV ads featuring rapist Willie Horton, an African American man who had attacked a woman while he was on a weekend leave from a prison in Massachusetts. Since the governor's office had signed off on the leave, Bush claimed that Dukakis had granted "a generous vacation to prisoners." The Bush ad campaign played on voter fears and prejudice.

PRESIDENT GEORGE H. W. BUSH
reads at his summer home in Maine.
Bush ran for president against
Michael Dukakis in 1988.

MICHAEL DUKAKIS *(right)* picked Texas senator Lloyd Bentsen to run as the Democratic vice presidential candidate in 1988.

Taxes figured uppermost in voters' minds, as they had in previous elections. Bush followed Reagan's lead and promised to cut taxes. He pledged, "Read my lips: no new taxes." Unable to counter Bush in a meaningful way on several fronts, Dukakis's campaign unraveled.

On November 8, 1988, voters elected George H. W. Bush as their forty-first president and former Indiana senator Dan Quayle as his vice president. Bush won by 53 percent of the popular vote to Dukakis's 46 percent. Bush was thrilled to become president. At his swearing in, he promised to use American strength as "a force for good."

Bush's leadership style differed from Reagan's in several ways. Reagan had preferred a detached leadership style, giving members of his administration free rein to execute his policies. Bush oversaw every detail. He also shunned the celebrity image that Reagan perfected. Instead, the more private Bush kept information within his close circle of friends. He preferred gathering facts from various sources and then making final decisions himself.

■ THE BREAKUP OF THE SOVIET UNION

Bush took office as the world was adjusting to the new order brought about by Gorbachev's glasnost. As U.S.-Soviet ties improved, the republics within the Soviet Union tested the limits of glasnost. In Poland Lech Walesa, a shipyard worker, had become the leader of a powerful labor union called Solidarity. (Although Poland no longer belonged to the Soviet Union, the Soviet Union controlled Poland's Communist government.)

The Berlin Wall stood as one of the most powerful symbols of Soviet Communism. The 100-mile (161-km) -long concrete wall stood between East and West Berlin, dividing the German city. The idea for the wall took root following World War II after the United States, France, Great Britain, and the Soviet Union conquered Germany. These Allies split Germany into four zones, including Berlin, the ruined German city. Zones held by western nations rebuilt quickly and thrived. But Moscow ran the eastern side as a Communist state, limiting development and prosperity. Berlin straddled the divide.

In 1949 separate governments for each side of Germany formed. Thousands of East Berliners fled to the West despite Soviet attempts to prevent travel. In 1961 the Soviet government erected a low barbed wire and brick wall between East and West Berlin to block people from leaving. Over the years, the Soviets made the wall stronger and higher. They added checkpoints, armed soldiers, guard dogs, and towers, all to keep the citizens of East Germany from escaping.

In 1987 President Reagan challenged his newfound friend Mikhail Gorbachev, the leader of the Soviet Union: "If you seek peace, if you seek prosperity for the Soviet Union and Eastern Europe, . . . Mr. Gorbachev, open this gate! Mr. Gorbachev, tear down this wall!"

A DEMONSTRATOR POUNDS AWAY AT THE BERLIN WALL in November 1989 as East Berlin border guards and onlookers watch.

In October 1989, after Reagan's presidency had ended, East Germans finally removed their Communist leaders from power. On November 9, 1989, East German leaders opened the Berlin Wall gates. A wild frenzy followed. East Germans swarmed into the streets to escape to the other side. Thrilled West Berliners welcomed them, searching for relatives and friends not seen since the war. "I just can't believe it," shouted one East Berlin woman. "I don't feel like I'm in prison anymore."

As crowds pushed through the gates, others scaled the wall. Excited East Germans attacked the hated wall with pick-axes and hammers. Everyone wanted a chunk of the wall as a souvenir. Within days, the unpopular symbol of repression had crumbled into a small pile of harmless bricks.

POLISH LABOR UNION LEADER LECH WALESA *(LEFT)* AND U.S. PRESIDENT GEORGE H. W. BUSH wave to the crowd in Gdansk, Poland, in July 1989.

Six months after Bush took office, Walesa forced the Polish government to restore the parliament and allow elections. Solidarity won a majority of the seats and led the government. A year later, Walesa became Poland's first president.

Poland's success swept through the Soviet-controlled nations of Eastern Europe like a runaway train. Poland had taken almost ten years to topple its Communist government. Those following in Poland's footsteps measured their success at overthrowing Communism in months (ten in Hungary), weeks (ten in East Germany), days (ten in Czechoslovakia), and hours (ten in Romania). After each revolt, these nations demanded the same liberty and independence enjoyed by Poland. Citizens experimented with free speech, free presses, and the ability to cross borders without fear of being shot. By 1990 Communism had lost its grip on Eastern Europe. Fifteen independent republics, including Russia, replaced the former Soviet Union. The mighty Soviet Union no longer existed.

By 1990 Communism had lost its grip on Eastern Europe.

Bush decided to maintain a strong military position while watching to see how the newly free former Soviet nations progressed. In the meantime, he turned his attention to Panama.

Bush feared that escalating violence put all Americans in Panama in danger. Further violence threatened to block free passage of vessels through the Panama Canal.

■ INVASION OF PANAMA

Before the 1988 presidential election, the Reagan administration had been secretly working with General Manuel Noriega, Panama's powerful military dictator. Noriega had helped supply arms to Nicaragua's contras during the Iran-contra affair. He had secretly been on the CIA's payroll since 1971, helping the United States by spying on neighboring nations in Central America. During Noriega's travels, though, he became involved in the profitable illegal drug trade.

In 1986 a journalist investigated reports that Noriega had given secret military information about the United States to Cuba. U.S. government efforts to stop Noriega failed. He threatened to expose meetings with Bush when he was CIA director, meetings Bush claimed never happened.

To avoid problems, Reagan had tried to cut a deal with Noriega, Reagan promised not to prosecute Noriega on drug charges if he would allow free elections in Panama in May 1989 and turn over the government to the winners of the election. Noriega canceled the election instead.

On December 16, 1989, four U.S. soldiers in Panama were attacked and one was shot. Bush feared that escalating violence put all Americans in Panama in danger. Further violence threatened to block free passage of vessels through the Panama Canal. The 10-mile-wide (16 km) channel, opened by the United States in 1914, saved ships traveling between the Atlantic and the Pacific oceans thousands of miles. If they couldn't pass through the canal, they would have to travel all the way around the South American continent.

On December 20, the president ordered 12,000 U.S. troops to invade Panama, seize Noriega, and protect the canal. Other Central American countries sharply protested the invasion, but Bush continued the assault. Panama's army resisted U.S. advances for four days before fighting ended. By then 23 Americans had died and 322 lay wounded. About 500 Panamanians had died, 3,000 were wounded, and tens of thousands of families had lost their homes.

A U.S. military helicopter flies over a burning building in **PANAMA CITY** on December 20, 1989. President George H. W. Bush sent troops into Panama despite opposition from some Central American countries.

On December 24, Noriega surrendered to U.S. soldiers. He was eventually tried and convicted on drug charges. The United States installed a new government in Panama and secured the canal.

DEMONSTRATORS PROTEST REAGAN'S ECONOMIC POLICIES—
sometimes called trickle-down economics—in the 1980s.

CHAPTER THREE

WEALTH AND POWER:
AN ECONOMIC REVOLUTION

When Reagan was elected president in 1980, he focused his attention on the nation's troubled economy. The cornerstone of Reagan's economic vision was lower taxes. He wanted to reduce the tax burdens of businesses and individuals, especially the rich. Reagan believed that if prosperous people and businesses paid lower taxes, they would invest their money instead of paying the government. Business owners might expand their businesses, while individuals might invest their money in the stock market. Reagan believed these investments would help the economy grow and create more jobs and higher wages for all workers. Economists called this concept trickle-down economics or supply-side economics. Political commentators began referring to it as Reagonomics.

The president's first budget called for cutting tax rates by a total of 30 percent over the next three years. Since the Treasury Department would lose this tax money, Reagan asked Congress to cut spending by $48.5 billion. As he proposed, social welfare programs suffered the greatest losses. Reagan requested cuts in food stamps, legal aid for the poor, and job training programs. He also requested cuts for federally funded school lunch programs. His administration offered the suggestion that ketchup be classified a vegetable to avoid the higher cost of real tomatoes. (That suggestion provided good material for comedians on radio and television.)

Additional cuts came from the budgets of agencies supporting the arts, mass transportation, and research on alternative types of fuels. Reagan had no intention of working to reduce U.S. dependence upon foreign oil, even though the high price of oil was contributing to the rising costs of goods and services. The military was the only department to escape cuts.

■ EFFECTS OF REAGONOMICS

A major problem with the U.S. budget was that it did not balance. Reagan asked the government to spend more money than came in through taxes and investments, which created a budget deficit. A deficit is the difference between the amount of money the government has in its treasury to pay for all of its programs and the much larger amount of money that it spends. The United States borrowed the additional money it needed from foreign nations. "I'm not worried about the deficit—it's big enough to take care of itself," Reagan joked.

On August 13, 1981, Congress rewarded Reagan with passage of the Economic Recovery Tax Act (ERTA), a sweeping overhaul of taxes. The final act met most of the president's demands. ERTA reduced income taxes by 28 percent over the next three years. It also reduced capital gains taxes by 40

Thousands of residents of Chicago, Illinois, **LINE UP FOR A FREE MEAL** at a Baptist church in the city in August 1982. The church provided meals and bags of food to many citizens experiencing hard times during the recession.

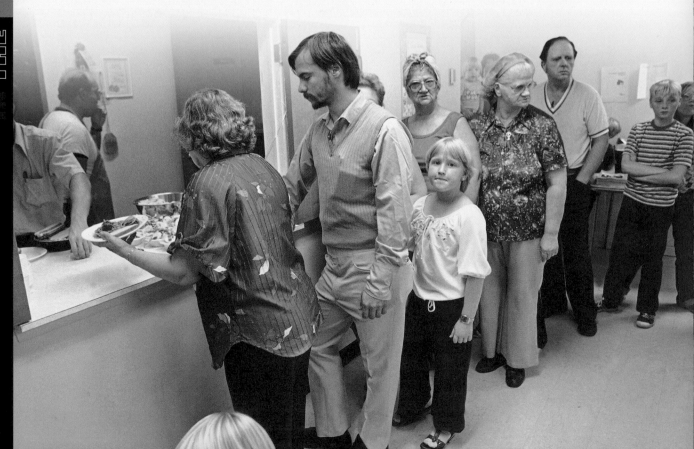

"Presidents don't create deficits. Congress does."

—Ronald Reagan, in his autobiography, 1990

percent. These are taxes that people pay on profits from investments such as stocks and bonds. Passage of the act represented the biggest tax cut in U.S. history. Conservatives, who disapprove of high taxes, were thrilled with their newfound power. Meanwhile, low-income people who looked to government for assistance felt betrayed.

Reagan's plan did not fix the economy. ERTA could do nothing about the steep rate of inflation. The average prices on goods that consumers and businesses purchased shot up by 12.5 percent. To fix the problem, the Federal Reserve Bank increased interest rates. The higher interest rates that businesses and individuals had to pay did help the inflation rate. But it also helped sink the country into a deep recession in 1982. By November 1982, nine million people in the United States had lost their jobs.

Meanwhile, Reagan's steep tax cuts and his huge increases in military spending increased the nation's budget deficit. The large deficit forced the government to borrow more money. It borrowed money from its citizens and from other countries. The national debt, which was the total amount the United States owed, skyrocketed. When criticized because his huge deficit made the economy worse, Reagan passed the responsibility for the problem onto Congress. "Presidents don't create deficits," he said, "Congress does."

■ THE RICH GET RICHER

By the time Reagan was up for reelection in 1984, the nation was climbing out of the recession. Inflation had plunged from 12.5 percent to 4.4 percent. And the unemployment rate—the percentage of working-age people without jobs—had fallen from 7.1 percent to 5.5 percent.

The recession had taken a big toll on people on the lowest rungs of the economic ladder. Reagan's budget cuts had shrunk unemployment payments for those who had lost their jobs and also for welfare payments for those who had little or no income. In addition, those with low-paying jobs saw their wages go down. The bottom 10 percent of households lost 10.5 percent of their income between 1977 and 1987.

	1980s	2000s (first decade)
Average U.S. worker's income	$15,757	$35,000

TYPICAL PRICES

Car	$6,495	$20,000
Bicycle	$110	$140
Movie Ticket	$3.55	$9.00
Half gallon of milk	$2.16	$2.40
Gallon of gas	$1.40	$2.00
Bottle of soda (1-liter)	98¢	$1
Candy bar	40¢	75¢
Loaf of bread	74¢	$2.79
First-class stamp	22¢	44¢
One-family house	$116,850	$300,000

(Prices are samples only. At any given time, prices vary by year, location, size, brand, and model.)

Meanwhile, the wealthiest 1 percent earned more than 90 percent of the nation's wealth. This meant that the 834,000 households at the top were worth nearly $6 trillion compared with nearly $5 trillion for the remaining 84 million U.S households. Reagan's idea that money to the rich "trickled down" to the poor never materialized. Homelessness soared as low-income family breadwinners lost jobs. By 1987, 20 percent of Americans lived in poverty. In the end, the rich got richer and the poor became poorer.

"As the rents went up, the wages of the working class stayed the same," the Reverend Patrick Mahoney told reporter Peter Jennings, "and suddenly many people couldn't afford to live in their own homes anymore. . . . The trickle-down theory just stopped at those who already had money. . . . It was tragic."

During his second term, Reagan called for additional tax reductions. In 1985 he submitted a one-trillion-dollar budget to Congress, which deepened the national debt. Reagan portrayed huge national debt and over-the-top spending as a sign of recovery, a good thing for the United States.

Many Americans embraced Reagan's buy now and pay later model. The use of credit cards soared. Economists began to call Reaganomics the "nation's charge-card economic recovery."

■ CORPORATE GREED

Many of the up-and-comers of the 1980s amassed their fortunes as lawyers, stock traders, accountants, or investment bankers. They used their skills to orchestrate company mergers (two companies joined together) or to repackage old businesses. They also dissolved companies, forcing them out of business. As reporter Peter Jennings wrote, they were "dealmakers interested not so much in making things as unmaking things, *rearranging* things and *putting them back together*." Investors encouraged corporate greed. Ivan Boesky was a company raider, who bought companies and sold them off quickly at a profit. "Greed is all right," Boesky said, " . . . everybody should be a little greedy."

For a time, U.S. laws provided checks against too much greed. In the late 1960s and 1970s, Congress had passed regulations to protect the environment and worker and consumer health and safety. Government supervised how banks and businesses kept their accounts and conducted operations. President Reagan sought to reduce these and other restrictions on businesses. He believed that instead of helping the public and the economy, regulations harmed them

IVAN BOESKY built a fortune in the 1980s from company mergers. In the mid-1980s, he was convicted of insider trading. He spent more than three years in prison for this illegal practice and became a symbol of corporate greed.

> **Reagan believed that instead of helping the public and the economy, regulations harmed them by keeping business from becoming profitable and creative.**

by keeping business from becoming profitable and creative.

During his first year in office, he froze new restrictions and worked to eliminate those already in place. He slashed staffs of the Consumer Product Safety Commission, Occupational Safety and Health Administration and of the Environmental Protection Agency. These agencies write and enforce regulations for corporations that safeguard against abuse. Reagan weakened rules of oversight in a range of businesses, including banks. The federal agencies were left with too few staff and little power to protect the public. Loosening rules that governed businesses, known as deregulation, gave investors more power. Workers and consumers were left with less.

■ BUYOUTS AND MERGERS

One company buying out another was not new. But in the 1980s, the deregulation of business sparked an avalanche of buyouts. Companies gobbled up others to improve their images, enlarge their product lines, or raise the value of their stocks for their investors. One of the larger mergers of the decade occurred when the R. J. Reynolds Tobacco Company

bought Nabisco Brands, of cookie and cracker fame, for $24.9 billion. Smoking and tobacco products were coming under fire for damaging health. Owning a cookie company softened the public's negative image of R. J. Reynolds as a business out to harm people.

During the 1980s, a new type of buyout reached its peak. It originated with investors who hoped to earn a quick profit rather than support a long-term business. They had little interest over the long haul in manufacturing products that customers would enjoy and buy. These corporate investors played their financial game by taking out large loans. Once they acquired a business, they streamlined it to turn greater profits so they could pay back their loans quickly. Investors sold off some of the company's profitable divisions or dissolved portions of the business altogether. After they earned enough money to repay their loans, investors often sold what was left of the business at a profit and searched for another company to buy for another fast dollar.

Mergers became so widespread they often changed the face of entire industries. During the 1980s, mergers of media companies reached epidemic proportions. In 1983 fifty corporations dominated mass media. Within four years, the number shrank to twenty-nine and dwindled to twenty-three by 1990.

■ PROBLEMS FOR WORKERS

Corporate wheeling and dealing took a toll on average workers. Investors sometimes overruled the decisions of a company's managers or made decisions that violated workers' union contracts. To improve profits, they often fired employees, no matter how long they had worked for the firm. Many workers who once counted on a lifetime of benefits with one company found themselves unemployed or working for less money in the same job or elsewhere.

Another problem, unrelated to buyouts and mergers, affected workers. The United States was importing more goods from other nations than buying goods produced by U.S. factories at lower prices. Americans began buying Japanese cars and clothes made in Taiwan, for example. As a result, the demand for U.S.-made cars, clothing, and other products shrank. This caused more layoffs and increased unemployment.

Layoffs and plant closings became common in many industries, such as automobile and steel production. Clothing and furniture industries suffered

AMERICAN WORKERS SUCH AS THIS WOMAN WERE IN DANGER OF LOSING THEIR MANUFACTURING JOBS in the 1980s because of buyouts and mergers. In addition, Americans were buying more imported goods, reducing the demand for American-made products.

STRIKING AIR TRAFFIC CONTROLLERS
protest in Detroit, Michigan, in 1981.

Unions lost considerable bargaining power to corporate management during the Reagan administration. Reagan's response when air traffic controllers walked off the job in 1981 signaled the change. The workers belonged to the Professional Air Traffic Controllers Organization (PATCO), a union of employees who guided planes in and out of airports safely. Controllers wanted a higher pay raise than the government offered and also less stressful work conditions. They claimed their current job hours and stress put air travelers in danger.

Reagan, a stickler for rules, remained unmoved by their demands. PATCO members were government workers and, as such, had given their word never to strike. Instead of meeting with union leaders, Reagan declared the strike illegal, fired all the workers, and found temporary replacements to keep the system working. He ordered the armed forces to keep airplanes flying until new workers received training. A chorus of supporters agreed with the president's decision.

Union leaders forecasted danger in the air without the controllers. They worried about accidents and poor service without expert direction from professional controllers. Critics charged the government had treated the union too harshly. But Reagan held firm, working to break the back of the union.

For a while, air travel slowed as new controllers were trained. In the end, working conditions for air traffic controllers returned to prestrike conditions. But the balance of power between employees and employers had shifted everywhere, giving management the upper hand. Employee unions could no longer count on government support. At the same time, Reagan bolstered his image as a tough leader who stood by his beliefs no matter what the cost.

slowdowns as manufacturing moved to countries where people worked for lower wages. Between 1981 and 1986, about five million longtime U.S. factory employees lost their jobs to plant closings or downsizing. Headlines trumpeted "Economic Recovery Is Seen as By-Passing at Least 10 Million."

> **"We're relearning the nature of debt. . . . Since October 19, 1987, there's been more and more talk about . . . having cash and not being in debt. . . . It used to be considered unethical to be deeply in debt. It showed a lack of discipline."**

—*novelist Tom Wolfe, 1989*

■ SAVINGS AND LOAN SCANDAL

Savings and loan (S&L) banks hold savings for average citizens and also lend them money for car loans, houses, or other small projects. Commercial banks, on the other hand, arrange for credit cards and business loans. Both types of financial institutions operate under strict government rules. Federal laws govern how and where they invest funds from their customers' savings account deposits to earn a profit. In exchange, the government maintains a special fund to protect a certain amount of money in each savings account in the event an S&L fails.

Savings and loans showed signs of problems during the 1960s and 1970s. In the early 1980s, the higher interest rates imposed by the Federal Reserve Bank hurt the S&Ls' already weak profits. On October 15, 1982, President Reagan signed into law a bill designed to help the ailing S&L industry. The Garn-St. Germain Depository Institutions Act, named for the two sponsoring congressmen, altered the banking industry by granting S&Ls new rights and protections. The act increased the amount of insured savings from forty thousand to one hundred thousand per account. This change freed S&Ls to take more risks when investing money elsewhere because government backed more of their accounts. The law also allowed control of S&Ls to rest in the hands of fewer directors.

The act granted S&Ls the ability to raise interest rates. This meant customer money in savings accounts received higher returns. In addition, S&Ls raised interest rates on loans to people who needed to borrow money. Because S&Ls got more money back for their loans, they were more willing to lend to riskier customers. More people acquired loans for houses and other projects.

Problems developed soon after the law passed. Drunk with greater freedom and without tight oversight, some S&Ls invested in a host of shady deals. According to one observer: "They [S&L directors] used money to buy themselves yachts, mansions and corporate jets. . . . They lost millions when they

Left to right, front: Senators John Glenn, Dennis DeConcini, and John McCain arrive at a Senate hearing in 1990. They were part of the Keating Five, five senators accused of intervening unethically in the investigation of a failing **SAVINGS AND LOAN BANK IN THE 1980S.** The scandal became a symbol of the S&L crisis.

speculated on race horses, windmill farms, exotic financial instruments, and chancy real estate ventures."

As stories of scandals and failed business ventures circulated, customers pulled their savings from S&Ls. Many of these banks, particularly those in Texas and California, went bankrupt trying to repay the accounts. Between 1986 and 1989, 296 S&Ls needed help returning money to customers with savings accounts. The federal insuring agency, the Federal Deposit Insurance Corporation (FDIC), normally covered losses. By 1989 the agency had run out of money.

As a result of the deepening crisis, Congress passed a resolution to use taxpayer money to save some of the S&Ls. For the first time, public tax money indirectly paid for the get-rich-quick schemes of financial institutions. The effects of the scandal lasted into the 1990s. By 1995, 1,043 financial institutions had closed. The cost to taxpayers had reached $153 billion. Several economists wrote, "The savings and loan crisis of the 1980s and early 1990s produced the greatest shrinking of U.S. financial institutions since the Great Depression."

■ BUSH INHERITS A MONEY MESS

George H. W. Bush entered office with a huge national debt problem. At $2.6 trillion, the nation's 1989 debt nearly tripled from the 1980 level. Complicating Bush's efforts to fix the economy was his campaign promise to trim the national debt without raising taxes.

Within a year, Bush went back on his pledge. On June 26, 1990, he released a statement saying, "It seems clear to me that both the size of the deficit problem and the need for a package that can be enacted [to stimulate the economy and lower national debt] required a number of measures, including tax revenue increases." The public outcry lasted Bush's entire term. Some say the decision cost him reelection.

By the 1980s, stock market prices had reached unusually high levels. On October 19, 1987, the market went into a nosedive. Many investors had decided that the stocks were not worth their asking prices, so they panicked and sold their stocks, sending stock prices in a downward spiral. The tumble represented losses of five hundred billion dollars for investors. October 19, 1987, became known as Black Monday.

Older Americans braced for a total collapse of the economy, which had occurred after the 1929 stock market crash. That market collapse plunged rich people into poverty and the nation into depression overnight. But the predicted total disaster never happened. Many people lost significant amounts of money in 1987, but the economy never collapsed completely.

Economists differed about what exactly caused the market collapse. Reagan's critics blamed him for spending money the government didn't have, creating huge budget deficits. They claimed those deficits had spread fear among investors that interest rates would rise steeply once again. So the investors sold their stocks. Others blamed stockbrokers' computers, which were programmed to automatically sell stocks for specific customers if the stocks dropped below a certain price. When the stock prices began falling, the computers automatically sold off a high volume of stocks, which made the situation worse.

Whatever the cause, the stock market bounced back and merger and buyout fever returned. A year after Black Monday, new investors took over RJR Nabisco, the company created from the merger of RJR tobacco and Nabisco foods. The investors bought the company for twenty-five billion dollars. The takeover became the most expensive in history.

Traders on the floor of the New York Stock Exchange work frantically as the markets plunge more than five hundred points on October 19, 1987.

49

Members of a LOCAL COMPUTER CLUB try out the keyboards on new Apple computers at a demonstration in San Francisco, California, in 1984.

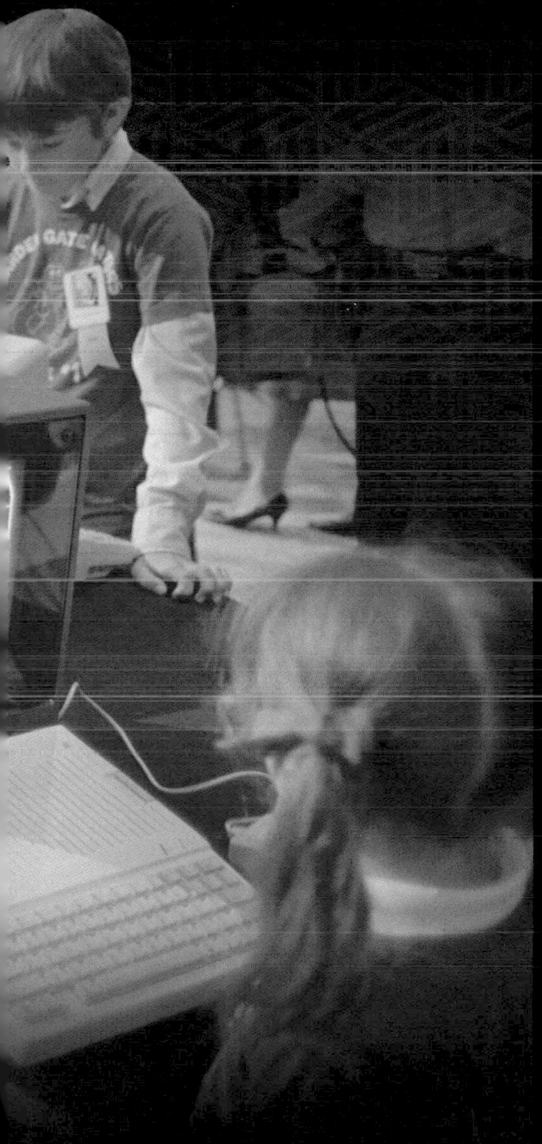

CHAPTER FOUR

BREAKING NEW GROUND:
SCIENCE, MEDICINE, AND TECHNOLOGY

During the 1980s, science and technology transformed the lives of many people in the United States. Improvements in computer technology and the arrival of the Internet revolutionized the way researchers at universities communicated with one another. Advances in medical technology made it possible for more couples to have children. Astronauts traveled to space in reusable shuttles. And some technology developed for space travel proved to be useful for civilians too.

■ THE EARLY HISTORY OF COMPUTERS

Some of the most exciting developments of the 1980s occurred in computer technology. Computers had been around for a while. During World War II, three members of the University of Pennsylvania's engineering school built a high-speed computer to make mathematical calculations for new U.S. military weapons systems. Each giant computer filled an entire room and housed eighteen thousand glass tubes to transmit electricity. Programmers made their calculations with the help of coded punched cards. These early computers

51

and their programs were limited in speed, scope, and memory. At first, only government and university research centers had the space, money, and professional skills to use computer technology.

In 1971 microprocessors made from tiny silicon chips replaced tubes. A microprocessor is a very small central processing unit, which is where the computer interprets instructions and carries out mathematical and other operations. The postage stamp-sized silicon chips allowed engineers to dream of making smaller personal computers.

The January 1975 issue of *Popular Electronics* featured the Altair 8800, thought to be the first personal computer. This and similar early personal computers were clunky machines without a keyboard, a monitor, or a mouse. A year later, William (Bill) Gates, a sophomore at Harvard University, and his childhood friend Paul Allen developed BASIC, an improved program language, or software, to run the Altair. Excited by computer technology, Gates and Allen left Harvard to form Microsoft, a software company for personal computers.

BILL GATES surrounded by computers in the early 1980s. Gates and his friend Paul Allen founded Microsoft, a computer software company, in 1977.

APPLE UNVEILED THE MACINTOSH COMPUTER in January 1984.

At around the same time, two other college dropouts, Stephen Wozniak and Steven Jobs, constructed a computer at Jobs's home in California. Their creation became the first Apple computer, later known as Apple I. The Apple I attracted a limited following at first, since early personal computers contained few of the advances that eventually made them useful. Still, the modest sales launched the Apple Company.

■ COMPUTER TECHNOLOGY MAKES BIG ADVANCES

In 1981 the technology giant International Business Machines (IBM) entered the personal computer market. Other electronics companies followed. Steven Jobs, a skilled marketer, donated Apple computers to schools. His bold move encouraged educators and parents to choose an Apple over the competition.

Over the next three years, Apple sold millions of computers and held 50 percent of the personal computer market. In 1984 Apple released the Macintosh, the first affordable computer to include graphics, a color monitor, keyboard, mouse, and floppy drive for 3.5-inch (8.9-centimeter) storage disks. This updated version was an instant success. Apple grew into a billion-dollar company.

While Apple improved its hardware and systems, other computer scientists explored software programs to make computers easier and faster to operate.

1980s

54

AMERICA IN THE

Steven Jobs was a bright, curious young man who used his talent and interests to create one of the first personal computers. Born in San Francisco in 1955 and adopted as an infant by Paul and Clara Jobs, Steven always loved electronics. While he was in high school, he met his future partner and engineering hotshot, Stephen Wozniak, while working during the summer for Hewlett-Packard.

After high school, Jobs attended Reed College in Oregon, but he dropped out. At first, he got a job designing computer games for Atari. Then he decided to create a personal computer anyone could operate. He coaxed Wozniak into providing the engineering know-how to help him build a personal computer. In 1975, with only thirteen hundred dollars, the two built their first product and managed to get the Byte Shop, a chain of computer stores, to order fifty computers. They assembled the computers in Jobs's garage. Jobs thought apples were the perfect fruit, so he and Wozniak named their business the Apple Computer and used an apple for the logo. They called their personal computer Apple I.

In 1984 Apple introduced the groundbreaking Macintosh. Customers loved a brand-new feature—a mouse. They used it to move the cursor and to click on an icon to open a program. The Macintosh was an instant success. By then computers had caught the imagination of a nation. On the cover of its January 3, 1983, issue, *Time*

STEVEN JOBS, founder of Apple Computer, in 1984

magazine called the computer the "Machine of the Year," a play on its usual "Man of the Year" January cover. President Reagan awarded Jobs and Wozniak the National Medal of Technology, the first ever given.

In 1985 Jobs, by then a multimillionaire, left Apple because of a disagreement. He started a new computer company, Next, Inc. A year later, he bought the computer graphics company Pixar Animation Studios, the company responsible for such animated hits as *Toy Story* (1995) and *Finding Nemo* (2003).

In 1997 Apple bought Next, Inc. As a result of the sale, Jobs returned to his original company and once again became its dynamic and creative leader. In 2001 Apple introduced the iPod, a portable music player. Two years later, along came iTunes, a virtual music store, and another big hit for Apple.

Jobs sold Pixar to the Walt Disney Company in 2006. He remains involved in its business as a board member and investor.

In 1980 Microsoft revolutionized computer use worldwide with the Windows operating system, which Bill Gates sold to IBM for all their computers. Windows provided uniform operations among computers that allowed users to work with text documents, accounting spreadsheets, and graphics. It also gave users the ability to dial into a worldwide computer network via telephone lines. Programs designed by Gates transformed personal computers into a must-have product for anyone who could spend between eleven hundred and two thousand dollars. By 1986 thirty-one-year-old Gates had become a billionaire.

Other companies added computer innovations. Hewlett-Packard introduced laser printers in 1985 and higher-quality monitors in 1986. The new printers boosted quality of reproductions over ink-jet printers. Graphics, memory management, typefaces, and networking capabilities improved at a rapid rate throughout the 1980s. By the end of the decade, computers recognized and responded to simple speech. These additions allowed buyers to use computers for a wider range of functions. Speed and memory improvements came so quickly that many computers became outdated every eighteen months. Still, only about 13 percent of the population owned a personal computer by the end of the decade.

HEWLETT-PACKARD representatives demonstrate a computer program in 1985.

THE INTERNET'S EARLY DAYS

Advanced computer technology laid the groundwork for a growing Internet communication system. The word *Internet* came from two words: *interconnected* and *network*. In the 1980s, the Internet connected individual computers to networks via telephone lines. Tiny threads called fiber-optic cables relayed information at rapid speeds. In the 1980s, most Internet users were government agencies and university research departments, which shared data and other information on the Internet.

In 1988 a commercial e-mail service provider, MCI Mail, received permission to link with the Internet. Soon other commercial e-mail service providers followed, clearing the way for business and ordinary citizens to connect with the Internet.

Investment in computer-related companies expanded. In the United States, the number of computer-related businesses mushroomed. Many opened in northern California. So many computer-related companies clustered in the stretch from Menlo Park south through San Jose that the region became known as Silicon Valley. San Jose called itself the Capital of Silicon Valley because of the large

number of technical labs and research centers there, including giants such as Hewlett-Packard and Adobe, a software creator.

Soon other commercial e-mail service providers followed, clearing the way for business and ordinary citizens to connect with the Internet.

TELEPHONE LINES HEAT UP

Computers were not the only new machine taking up space in offices and at home in the 1980s. Businesses began using smaller, faster models of telefax, or fax, machines. These machines scan letters, documents, and other printed information and transmit the information across telephone lines to the recipient's fax machine, which may be across town or across the ocean. The recipient's fax machine prints a copy. By 1980 most of these machines conformed to the same standard, which made it possible for them to communicate with one another.

Cordless phones appeared in the 1980s too, although many callers had to ignore the conversations these

CORDLESS PHONES, such as the one this student is using, were first introduced in the 1980s.

units picked up from a neighbor's line. The first handheld commercial mobile phone arrived in stores in 1984. But few customers could afford its hefty $3,995 price tag.

Americans have always prided themselves on innovation. The number of patents registered with the U.S. government for technology-related inventions skyrocketed between 1977 and 1989. Patents protect owners from other people copying and making money off an invention for twenty years from the date of application.

At one time, invention patents went mostly to individuals who were U.S. citizens. But in the 1980s, corporations, including many from overseas, applied to control the commercial use of their employees' inventions. The increasing number of foreign countries wanting U.S. patents reflected the growing global economy. However, the United States still provided leadership in computers, medical science, and space travel.

■ THE REUSABLE SPACE SHUTTLE

The National Aeronautics and Space Administration (NASA), the U.S. government space program, had been using computers to help send humans into outer space since before the first moon landing in 1969. Each advance in computer technology helped NASA overcome some of the challenges of space exploration and travel.

Space technology, in turn, produced advances in other fields. For example, astronauts wore a portable cooling system of liquid-filled garments under their space suits to protect them against the moon's hot surface. In 1982 this technology became available to treat medical problems, such as severe burns and spine injuries. In 1986 lightweight breathing devices used by astronauts were made available to firefighters.

A major breakthrough in space travel occurred in the 1980s with the development of space shuttles. A shuttle is a reusable spacecraft launched into space by rockets on the ground. When the shuttle returns to Earth, it lands on a runway smoothly like an airplane. This unique ability to land on a runway meant shuttles could be reused, unlike previous spacecraft.

The shuttle was designed to eventually transport, or shuttle, freight between Earth and a space station already in orbit. Shuttles could carry up to 14 tons (13 metric tons), the weight of about two adult African elephants. The shuttle's ability to carry heavy loads allowed astronauts to return disabled satellites to Earth if they could not be repaired in space. Each shuttle cost about $5.5 trillion. NASA believed space shuttles would prove safe enough to one day carry paying private travelers.

The first shuttle, the *Columbia*, rose from a Florida launchpad on April 12, 1981. The practice run

lasted thirty-six hours and fifty-four minutes. Afterward, the shuttle made a smooth landing in California. Four more shuttle test flights succeeded, which was a triumph for space travel and exploration.

■ THE TRAGIC FLIGHT OF THE *CHALLENGER*

Despite the success of the shuttle program, by 1981 the public was losing interest in space travel. Some lawmakers and citizens questioned the high cost of NASA projects during the recession, when so many people desperately needed government help on Earth.

To renew interest in its space program, NASA introduced a series of publicity events. On June 18, 1983, NASA sent physicist Dr. Sally Ride into space on the *Challenger*. She became the first American woman to travel in space. From August 30 through September 5, 1983, Lt. Colonel Guion Bluford Jr., the first African American in space, traveled on the *Challenger*. This same trip included Dr. William Thornton, at the age of fifty-four, the oldest U.S. astronaut to experience space travel.

In 1986 NASA prepared its biggest media-grabbing spectacle. NASA gathered a diverse crew of six astronauts to fly on the *Challenger*, including a Japanese American man, an African American man, and two women. The seventh crew member was Christa McAuliffe, a thirty-seven-year-old social studies teacher from Concord, New Hampshire. NASA chose McAuliffe from more than eleven thousand applicants to be the first private U.S. citizen in space. She planned to teach two fifteen-minute classes from the *Challenger*, which would be broadcast into classrooms nationwide. A new generation of students would see the inside of a shuttle, catch a glimpse of an astronaut's life, and learn that, one day, they could travel through space.

On the morning of January 28, millions of television viewers, many of them schoolchildren, tuned in to watch the launch. Several thousand people, including McAuliffe's family, stood on the cold Florida field at Cape Canaveral to watch the shuttle liftoff.

At first, the liftoff appeared to go as planned. The shuttle took off at 1,977 miles (3,182 km) per hour. Less than two minutes after takeoff, however, sparks flashed from the spacecraft. Something seemed terribly wrong. A trail of smoke blurred people's vision from the ground. Then the shuttle exploded into a fiery ball. All seven crew members died instantly.

IN 1986 *CHALLENGER* CREW MEMBER CHRISTA McAULIFFE became the first private U.S. citizen in space.

❝ I want to say something to the school children . . . who were watching the live coverage of the shuttle's takeoff. I know it is hard to understand, but sometimes painful things like this happen. It's all part of the process of exploration and discovery. . . . The future doesn't belong to the fainthearted; it belongs to the brave. The *Challenger* crew was pulling us into the Future, and we'll continue to follow them.❞

—President Ronald Reagan, 1983

Hours after the explosion, President Reagan addressed a shocked and saddened nation. Memorial services were held throughout the country. Teachers, principals, and parents everywhere tried to help children find a way to make sense of the tragedy they had witnessed. "Someone they admired and loved has been taken away," explained the principal at McAuliffe's high school. ". . . [and] they have learned that nothing in this life is certain."

The disaster was the largest loss of life in space travel history. NASA had launched fifty-five missions without a significant problem. But a leak inside one of the *Challenger*'s booster rockets shattered the United States' confidence in its ability to explore space. President Reagan refused to scrap the shuttle program. Instead, he ordered NASA to check and repair every inch of the next shuttle before launching another mission. In 1988 the space program resumed with the launch of the *Discovery* shuttle.

Smoke trails filled the sky after **THE SPACE SHUTTLE** *CHALLENGER* **EXPLODED** on January 28, 1986.

■ MEDICAL BREAKTHROUGHS

Like space travel and computer technology, medical science conquered new frontiers during the 1980s. On December 2, 1982, a surgeon replaced the two ventricles of a patient's heart with an aluminum and plastic device. The device, called the Jarvik-7, was named for its inventor, Robert K. Jarvik. It imitated the pumping action of the patient's own ventricles, which no longer functioned properly. The patient, a dentist named Barney Clark, lived for 112 days. The experiment encouraged doctors everywhere to believe that someone would eventually design an artificial heart that would last a lifetime.

In the 1980s, medical science also offered a helping hand to couples unable to conceive a child on their own. In 1984 the first baby created from a donated egg was born. Doctors collected eggs from one woman, the donor. In a laboratory, they fertilized the eggs with sperm from the future father. Then they implanted the fertilized eggs into the uterus of the future mother.

In some cases, biological parents contracted with another woman to give birth to their child. This carrier, known as a surrogate, allowed an embryo to be implanted in her uterus for a fee. She carried the fetus to term (usually nine months) and gave the baby to its parents upon birth. Surrogates could be the source of the egg or not. By 1987 about five hundred American babies had been born under similar arrangements.

In 1984 Harvard scientists created a mouse in a laboratory from the cells of another mouse. The procedure, called cloning, resulted in a mouse that was identical to the one from which it was cloned.

That same year, a fifteen-day-old baby known as Baby Fae received the heart of a baboon. Although she lived less than three weeks with her new heart, her surgery added to the moral issues troubling those concerned about medical ethics. How far should scientists go to save or create life? Should humans have animal body parts? Whose baby is it when a surrogate mother gives birth to a baby?

■ IDENTIFYING THE AIDS EPIDEMIC

In 1981 doctors noticed that some patients displayed similar patterns of puzzling symptoms. Their unusual infections refused to clear up. Patients seemed tired and lost weight quickly. Some developed rare cancers. As doctors tracked the number of reported cases, they saw shocking figures. The numbers doubled every five months. By early 1983, health authorities counted thirteen hundred known cases of the mysterious disease and believed that countless others went unreported. People were dying, but no one knew why. In the United States, homosexual men and drug addicts seemed to be the most frequent victims. But in Africa, the illness was also showing up among women and among people who did not use drugs.

In April 1984, scientists in the United States and France, each working separately, announced a breakthrough in research into the disease. They identified the human immunodeficiency virus (HIV), which caused the condition. Because the virus attacked the body's immune system, which fights off diseases, they called the illness acquired immunodeficiency syndrome, or AIDS.

After researchers isolated the virus, they devised a blood test to identify infected patients. Doctors found that individuals could have the virus for ten years or more without showing symptoms. They also discovered that a person gets AIDS by coming in contact with the body fluids of someone who has the disease. For example, a drug addict might get it by using a hypodermic needle that has already been used by someone with AIDS. Having sex with an infected person is another way. A pregnant woman with AIDS can pass the virus to the embryo developing in her body.

Some health professionals focused on preventing HIV from spreading. Surgeon General Dr. C. Everett Koop issued a report calling for education concerning AIDS to be offered in schools "at the lowest grade possible as part of any health and hygiene program." He encouraged the use of condoms as a way to prevent the spread of HIV through sexual activity. Discussions about condoms and sexual relations became common in many public high schools. By the end of the

Doctors examine an **AIDS PATIENT** at a hospital in New York in 1989.

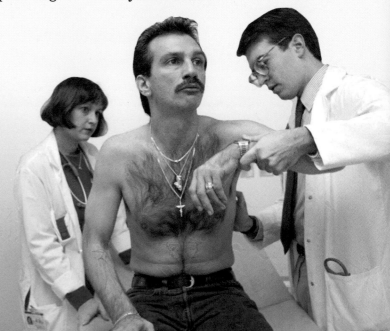

]n 1985 the Kokomo, Indiana, school district barred thirteen-year-old Ryan White from attending class because he had AIDS. Ryan was born with hemophilia, a disorder that prevents blood from clotting. When he had a wound, Ryan often required a blood transfusion—blood injected into his system through a needle—to heal. One transfusion accidentally contaminated Ryan's blood with the HIV virus. As a result, Ryan got AIDS.

His neighbors panicked. People feared catching AIDS through the air Ryan breathed or by touching him, even though medical research suggested this kind of transmission was impossible. Ryan's school banned him from coming into the building. He received his seventh-grade education at home. Ryan's teachers communicated with him by telephone.

The fearful community threatened the White family. Townspeople broke their house windows, punctured their car tires, and shot a bullet through their living room window. The family eventually had to move to protect their safety. "All I wanted

RYAN WHITE helped educate people about living with AIDS.

was to go to school and fit in," Ryan told reporters.

Ryan's ordeal attracted national media attention. He welcomed the chance to help other children with AIDS. He appeared on talk shows, attended fund-raisers, and addressed a White House hearing about AIDS. By going public, Ryan helped average Americans understand that anyone could get AIDS. Music celebrities, such as Elton John and Michael Jackson, befriended Ryan. They appeared with him to dispel the fear that people could get AIDS by touching someone with the disease.

On April 8, 1990, Ryan died. Fifteen hundred people packed his funeral, some of them famous. They came to honor the courageous boy who opened doors of hope for other children with AIDS.

63

1980s, almost one hundred nations reported cases of AIDS, and the number of cases continued to rise rapidly. The U.S. death toll from AIDS was close to one hundred thousand. Many Americans knew someone touched by the disease.

Sun City, Arizona, was one of many U.S. SUBURBS that had population growth spurts in the 1980s.

CHAPTER FIVE

CHANGING FACE OF AMERICA:
FAMILIES, NEIGHBORHOODS, AND SOCIETY

The U.S. population grew from 227 million in 1980 to 247 million in 1990. As the population grew, it also moved around. Many families moved from cities to the suburbs, a trend that had begun in previous decades. Americans also moved from colder climates to warm southern and southwestern states, which became known as the Sun Belt. Some had retired from their jobs. Others were looking for better job opportunities. Sun Belt cities such as Houston, Texas; Phoenix, Arizona; and Atlanta, Georgia, blossomed. Meanwhile, old northern cities such as Pittsburgh, Pennsylvania, and Buffalo, New York, which were once manufacturing centers, shrank as companies moved south or went out of business. Of the ten largest U.S. cities in 1900, only three, Chicago, Philadelphia, and New York, made the list in 1990.

Former professional football player and actor Terry Crews grew up in Flint, Michigan, where his father was a foreman at a General Motors plant. When the automobile industry slumped and plants closed during the 1980s, the population of Flint shrank dramatically. "We went from ten high schools to three," Crews recalled. "Everyone left. There were no jobs."

■ HARDER TIMES FOR MANY FAMILIES

During the 1980s, the United States was home to millions of working poor, people with jobs and low income. In 1982 more than 2.1 million people lived below the poverty line. For a family of four, the poverty line was a household income of $11,200. Many adults worked more than one job to keep the family afloat.

Author Barbara Ehrenreich wrote about problems facing the working poor and the middle class: "Whole occupational groups and subpopulations—farmers, steelworkers, single mothers—began to tumble toward the bottom. Other groups—office workers, schoolteachers, even higher-status professionals and their families—found themselves scrambling to remain in place."

Women went to work in greater numbers in the 1980s. In many families, women brought home a second paycheck, in addition to their husband's, which no longer seemed like enough. But an increasing number of families were headed by only one parent, often the mother. In 1970 married couples headed about 71 percent of families. By 1989 the number had dropped to about 57 percent.

Women went to work in greater numbers in the 1980s. In many families, women brought home a second paycheck, in addition to their husband's, which no longer seemed like enough.

■ WOMEN IN THE WORKPLACE

During the 1960s and 1970s, women demanded equality in the workplace and in colleges and universities. By the 1980s, women enjoyed more opportunities in both places. Advanced programs at institutions for higher education became more accessible to women. More of them trained to become lawyers and doctors, which were traditionally male professions.

Before 1970 few women entered programs for PhDs, the highest degree universities offer. Every year since, the number of women granted this degree rose by more than 1 percent. By 1985 women represented almost 30 percent of all PhD degrees. Medical and pharmacy schools enrolled eight men for every one woman before 1975. Ten years later, the ratio had narrowed to two men for every one woman. The women who earned advanced degrees in historic numbers went on to change the face

ELIZABETH DOLE was secretary of transportation in Reagan's cabinet from 1983 to 1987. She was the first woman to serve in that role.

of the nation's workforce. They became business executives, elected officials, doctors, lawyers, and engineers.

Ronald Reagan never truly embraced full equality for women. But he became the first president to appoint three women to high-level government posts, in addition to nominating Sandra Day O'Connor for the Supreme Court. Elizabeth Dole joined the Reagan cabinet as secretary of transportation. Margaret Heckler became secretary of health and human services, and Jeane Kirkpatrick represented the United States at the United Nations.

Many women felt they had to choose between a career and family, and they were torn. They knew they had to work harder and longer hours to get the job promotions they wanted. But they also felt they should go home to help their children with homework and drive them to sports games and other activities.

The media seemed to reinforce how unhappy working moms were. Reports charged that top jobs were coming at a price for many women. Critics accused working mothers of not caring about their children and letting nannies, day care centers, preschools, or after-school programs raise them. The media said that working women were burned out. The media attacked single professional women too. Articles recounted how single career women were "grieving from a man shortage" and were lonely.

Despite the gains that women made in high-paying professional fields, most remained stuck in traditionally female, low-wage office, teaching, sales, or service work. Three in every four working women made less than twenty thousand dollars per year. Even those in professional jobs took home an average of fifty-seven cents for every dollar a man earned. Black and Latina women suffered the widest income gaps, earning far less than men for similar jobs.

On March 22, 1972, Congress passed the Equal Rights Amendment (ERA). It would have been the twenty-seventh amendment to the Constitution if it had been ratified (approved) by thirty-eight states, as the law requires. The wording of the amendment had not changed since Alice Paul first wrote it in 1923. It read, "Equality of rights under the law shall not be denied or abridged by the United States or by any state on account of sex." The sentence affirmed equal rights for women under the law. Amendment supporters hoped that once it became part of the Constitution, federal and state governments would have to get rid of laws that discriminated against women. The National Organization for Women (NOW) led the drive to get the amendment passed.

By the time Reagan became president, thirty-five states had ratified the amendment. The Republican Party and the president opposed the ERA, and so did a lot of other Americans. States' rights supporters believed each state should decide whether to grant women equal rights, without any interference from the federal government. Ultrareligious groups feared that if the amendment became law, women might abandon their traditional roles as wives and mothers. Some opponents claimed the amendment would deny women financial support from their ex-husbands should they divorce. Others charged that women

NOW president Eleanor Smeal led the organization to work for passage of the EQUAL RIGHTS AMENDMENT in the 1980s.

would be sent into combat at a time when few women were entering the military.

"My feeling about the amendment is... it would eliminate those laws we now have which recognize the physical differences between men and women," Reagan declared.

ERA supporters fought back. They lobbied Congress, marched in Washington, D.C., and state capitals, and petitioned state lawmakers. Some women went on hunger strikes. Despite these efforts, they were unable to get three more states to ratify the amendment by the 1982 deadline. The defeat of the ERA put an end to the momentum of the women's movement, which had begun decades earlier. But committed women announced the struggle for equal rights would continue. Each year since then, the amendment has been reintroduced in Congress but without success.

■ SOME AFRICAN AMERICANS CLIMB HIGHER AND OTHERS SLIP

African Americans were about 12 percent of the U.S. population in the 1980s. Most hoped the significant gains they had made during the 1960s and 1970s would continue, and in many ways, that proved to be true. They continued to achieve a higher level of education, and the range of job opportunities for educated African Americans increased. Forty percent of college-educated blacks held professional jobs in 1980. In 1988 that number increased to 50 percent. A new generation of black professional business owners emerged. As a result of their success in business and in professions, many African Americans could afford to leave the inner cities for suburbs with better schools and housing.

JOB OPPORTUNITIES FOR COLLEGE-EDUCATED AFRICAN AMERICAN MEN AND WOMEN increased in the 1980s.

1980s

70

AMERICA IN THE

Dr. Martin Luther King Jr. began his careers as a minister and a civil rights leader in Montgomery, Alabama. He had been minister of a Baptist church for less than a year when on December 1, 1955, Rosa Parks refused to move to the back of a segregated bus (where blacks sat) in Montgomery. Back then local laws prohibited African Americans from using the same water fountains, schools, and other public facilities as whites. African Americans sought to overturn these discriminatory laws. In response to Parks's arrest, King launched a yearlong boycott of the city's buses. The boycott ended when the Supreme Court ruled that segregation on public buses was unconstitutional. The boycott's success helped stimulate the civil rights movement and made King one of its national leaders.

After the boycott, King founded the Southern Christian Leadership Conference (SCLC). As its president, he continued his nonviolent push for civil rights. In 1963 King organized the March on Washington. He rallied the two hundred thousand blacks and whites in the audience, with his historic "I have a dream" speech. On April 4, 1968, an assassin's bullet robbed the civil rights movement of its greatest leader.

Four days after King's murder, U.S. representative John Conyers of Michigan introduced a bill to create a federal holiday to honor King's memory. More than six million people signed petitions in support. Some members of Congress balked at the idea, saying there were many who worked for civil rights. Illinois did not wait for congressional approval. It passed a law declaring a state holiday on January 15, King's birthday.

Years after Conyers's bill first stalled in Congress, Conyers and New York representative Shirley Chisholm tried again to honor King with a national holiday. (Chisholm was the first African American woman elected to Congress.) Many congressional representatives and senators continued to oppose it. They said their main objection was that the holiday was so close to Christmas and New Years. But the real reason was lingering prejudice against blacks among residents of their states.

Chisholm and Conyers offered to move the date from King's birthday to a Monday later in January. This offer left the opposition without a good reason to explain their objections. In 1983 Congress passed a bill making the third Monday in January Martin Luther King Day. Although some states resisted, by 1989 forty-four states had adopted Martin Luther King Day as a holiday. This national holiday marked the first such day to honor an African American.

But during the downturn in the nation's economy during the early 1980s, African Americans without a college education suffered more than white people without a college degree. The number of manufacturing jobs declined, leaving many black people in that sector jobless and without options. Job training programs and low-income housing, which had helped African Americans in previous decades, shrank or disappeared because of federal budget cuts. At the same time, the Reagan administration had lost interest in enforcing laws that gave blacks equal access to jobs and educational opportunities. Therefore, fewer minorities won discrimination lawsuits. Many black families lost their place in the middle class.

■ JUST SAY NO!

Many jobless men and women of all races fell into despair. Drug use increased in the inner cities. In the mid-1980s, crack, a highly addictive form of cocaine, added to the problems of urban areas. Crack was the poor person's version of regular cocaine, and it made users into addicts almost from the first hit. Addicts needed about one thousand dollars a month to support their habit. Desperate men and women sometimes became criminals in their search for enough money. Some could no longer afford to pay their rent and lost their homes. According to one study, two-thirds of single men and women occupying New York City shelters for the homeless used crack.

First Lady Nancy Reagan campaigned to persuade the nation's youth to turn their backs on drugs. In 1983 she unveiled her "Just Say No" program. She urged schools to use the slogan when educating teenagers about how to avoid crack and other illegal drugs. Many thought the program was simplistic and did not have enough muscle to tackle a nationwide epidemic.

FIRST LADY NANCY REAGAN ATTENDS A "JUST SAY NO" program at a school in the 1980s. The First Lady worked to educate teenagers about the dangers of drug abuse.

■ THE NEWEST IMMIGRANTS

In the 1980s, immigration to the United States rose sharply. According to the U.S. Census Bureau, about six million people immigrated to the United States legally. About two million more entered illegally, below the radar of immigration officials. Almost half came from Latin American and Caribbean countries. The greatest number of Latino immigrants left homes in Mexico to escape grinding poverty and unemployment there. Another 40 percent of those who immigrated to the United States came from Asian countries. They came from Vietnam and Laos, where wars had produced many refugees, and from the Philippines, Korea, and India. By the end of the decade, about twenty million Latinos and about seven million Asians and Asian Americans lived in the United States.

The nation's large immigrant population presented educators with challenges. They debated whether to teach immigrant children in their own languages in separate classes or to include them in standard classes taught in English and give them extra help. Some overwhelmed urban schools left these students to fend for themselves.

■ BACK TO BASICS

During the 1980s, many urban schools declined. By then middle-class families, most of them white, had moved to the suburbs. White flight left growing poor and immigrant populations in the city school systems. As the student popula-

WITH RISING IMMIGRATION IN THE 1980s, U.S. classrooms, such as this one in Washington, D.C., became more diverse.

> ** " I would like each child to be seen as a very precious individual . . . in every class. If they're black, if they're Hispanic, value them for that—don't see it as a second-class status. "**

—*T. Berry Brazelton, pediatrician, 1989*

tion changed, critics complained that urban public school teachers didn't know how to teach their students. In 1983 a report issued by the National Commission on Excellence in Education announced that students in schools around the country were achieving less, and not just in urban areas. In addition, fewer students were graduating from high school.

In 1985 President Reagan appointed the conservative educator William Bennett to become secretary of education and take charge of improving the nation's schools. Bennett introduced the idea of regular nationwide testing of teachers and students. He urged public school teachers to spend more time on basic subjects, such as reading and math, and less on music and art, which he thought were frivolous. The secretary of education also proposed giving money to dissatisfied parents who wanted to send their children to private or religious schools. The money was called a school voucher. Debates over national testing and school vouchers continued for decades.

William Bennett thought it was fine for religious groups to have a say in what children learned in school. The growing voice of religious conservatives helped triple the rate of books banned from school and public libraries during the 1980s.

Adults removed these books from school and public libraries for any number of reasons. The books that were frequently banned included Mark Twain's *The Adventures of Huckleberry Finn*, for a tone that struck some groups as racist; Judy Blume's *Are You There God? It's Me, Margaret* and *Forever*, for their frank discussions of adolescent behavior; and even the *American Heritage Dictionary*, because it contained offensive words.

■ AN ERA OF BIG-BOX STORES AND SHOPPING MALLS

With both parents working in many families, moms and dads had trouble finding enough time to care for their children, shop for groceries and other items, cook, and clean the house. Time became a critical factor in many people's lives. Any company that helped working families save time got business.

73

For example, in the 1980s, customers significantly increased their visits to fast-food restaurants and drive-through car washes and banks.

Big-box stores and shopping malls had been around for a while. But as time became more precious in the 1980s, they mushroomed across the nation. Big-box stores are huge windowless warehouses of between 50,000 and 200,000 square feet (4,600 and 18,600 sqare meters) of merchandise space, which are surrounded by giant parking lots. Many specialize in one type of product. Home Depot sells household and do-it-yourself products. Some big-box chains, such as Wal-Mart, sell a variety of goods. National chain stores buy their products directly from manufacturers, rather than from wholesale distributors. By cutting out these wholesalers, big-box stores can offer lower prices to customers than can smaller, privately owned stores.

Like big-box stores, shopping malls grew dramatically during the 1980s. Shopping malls help busy customers by gathering many stores in one location or under one roof and providing easy parking nearby. Shopping malls had been around since the early 1900s. But in the 1980s, shopping malls entered

Shoppers crowd Harbor Place, an **INDOOR SHOPPING MALL** on the waterfront in Baltimore, Maryland, in 1981.

a boom phase. Sixteen thousand new ones were established. For the first time, many malls expanded to more than 800,000 square feet (74,300 sq. m). In addition to stores, they included restaurants and sometimes movie theaters.

The combined draw of big-box stores and shopping malls proved so great that 280 Metro Center in Colma, California, succeeded even though the center opened near a cemetery. Jokes about the location prompted the popular phrases "Shop till you drop" and "Shop a lot, buy a plot."

As customers flocked to suburban malls, fewer people purchased goods in smaller shops in town. Within a short time after opening, big-box stores and large malls drew customers away from independently owned, family-run stores. Many of them closed, leaving town centers with empty storefronts.

■ ENTER THE YUPPIES

Not everyone was shopping at economical big-box stores such as Wal-Mart or chain stores at the mall. Some young adults who became wealthier during the 1980s preferred more exclusive shops. Their glitzy lifestyle—clothes, cars, and everything else—caught the nation's attention.

The San Francisco writer Alice Kahn noticed these successful professionals moving into her neighborhood. She gave them the nickname yuppies, for *young, urban professionals*, and the name stuck. Kahn's new neighbors tended to be workaholic (addicted to working long hours) single adults with good job prospects and the hopes of earning fat paychecks.

Advertisers targeted yuppies to sell their products. In 1985 *Newsweek* made yuppies the subject of a cover story. The magazine reported that yuppies represented about four million young urban professionals between the ages of twenty-five and thirty-nine.

"They did not study; they 'networked.' They did not save; they spent," noticed author Barbara Ehrenreich. "And they did not spend on houses or station wagons but on Rolex watches, Porsches, quick trips to Aruba, and . . . high-status foods."

By the end of the decade, the yuppies' image had soured. They became the objects of scorn because of their self-centered, binge-buying lifestyles. Author Tom Wolfe called them the "Me! Me! Me!" generation.

This newstand in New York City shows a DIVERSE COLLECTION OF MAGAZINES in the 1980s. The decade saw a rise in the number of new magazines that targeted niche audiences.

CHAPTER SIX

THE WRITTEN WORD:

LITERATURE AND JOURNALISM IN THE 1980S

D uring the 1980s, adult book lovers' tastes ranged from Anne Tyler's literary novels to the autobiography of Lee Iacocca, the famously successful head of the Chrysler Corporation. Their daughters, meanwhile, enjoyed Ann Martin's series The Baby-Sitters Club. And there seemed to be a magazine to please just about everyone, from computer geeks to young sports fans.

■ TOP-SELLING BOOKS

In the 1980s, readers continued buying self-help books, a category that had become popular during the 1970s. A constant stream of diet books, such as *Never-Say-Diet Book* (1980) by the exercise guru Richard Simmons and *The Beverly Hills Diet* (1981) by Judy Mazel, sold to those in pursuit of the perfect body.

Other readers were more interested in perfecting their management style or improving their business. One of the first major management books to gain attention was Thomas Peters and Robert Waterman Jr.'s 1982 *In Search of Excellence: Lessons from America's Best-Run Companies*. After reviewing forty-three successful U.S. companies, the authors identified eight principles for managing a business. In the same year, Kenneth Blanchard and Spencer Johnson published *The One Minute Manager*, about how to achieve prosperity and job satisfaction.

77

The biggest business-oriented hit of the decade was Lee Iacocca's 1984 *Iacocca: An Autobiography*. Iacocca was known beyond the business community for his television pitches on behalf of Chrysler cars. His rags-to-riches story about how he created Ford's Mustang and went on to save Chrysler Motors from going out of business impressed thousands of readers.

Some nonfiction authors added some humor to their advice. Comedian, actor, and educator Bill Cosby taught families how to bring up responsible children with his 1986 *Fatherhood*. Henry Beard's 1981 *Miss Piggy's Guide to Life* used humor about the famed Muppet puppet to urge readers to get in touch with their inner feelings. Robert Fulghum simplified the road to self-improvement with his best-selling 1988 book *All I Really Need to Know I Learned in Kindergarten*. And Lisa Birnbach's 1980 *Official Preppy Handbook* spoofed the fashion tastes and lifestyles of people who had attended exclusive private high schools, known as "prep schools" (short for preparatory schools).

While readers turned to experts for advice, they looked to novelists for literary enrichment and sometimes for the joy of mental escape. Tom Wolfe created a stir with his 1987 novel *The Bonfire of the Vanities*. It skewered the greedy ambitions of a man who worked in the lofty heights of the financial world in New York City. The novel became a hit movie in 1990, with Tom Hanks as lead actor.

Another novel made into a movie was Anne Tyler's *The Accidental*

LEE IACOCCA wrote a popular book in 1984 about his life in the auto industry.

Tourist. Three years after its 1985 publication, this story about love and loss appeared in movie theaters. Tyler's novel *Breathing Lessons*, which appeared in 1988, won the prestigious Pulitzer Prize.

Scott Turow, a lawyer turned author, introduced a new type of detective story with his 1987 novel *Presumed Innocent*. The story and characters exposed flaws in the legal profession and paved the way for other legal thrillers, such as those by John Grisham. At the same time, more traditional mysteries, horror stories, and romance novels remained popular. Books by Tom Clancy (military thrillers), John le Carré (spy novels), Stephen King (horror), and Danielle Steele (romance) sold in the millions.

More than in previous decades, African American authors climbed the best-seller lists too. Toni Morrison received a Pulitzer Prize for Fiction for her 1987 novel *Beloved*, based on the true story of an escaped slave who killed her child rather than return her to slavery. Another novel that focused on racial inequality was Alice Walker's *The Color Purple* (1982). In 1983 the novel earned Walker the Pulitzer Prize for Fiction and the National Book Award. Director Steven Spielberg turned the story into a movie with Danny Glover and Whoopi Goldberg in 1985.

Gwendolyn Brooks, the first black to earn a Pulitzer Prize for Poetry, saw eight volumes of her poetry and prose appear during the 1980s. Other eminent poets whose books were published that decade included Robert Creeley, Robert Penn Warren, Louise Glück, and Donald Hall.

Toni Morrison has had a long and acclaimed career in writing. Born Chloe Anthony Wofford in Lorain, Ohio, in 1931, Morrison came from a family proud of their southern black roots. Morrison's mother often shared folk tales with her children. But she also told stories of the discrimination the family had experienced in the South.

An honors high school student, Morrison went on to attend Howard University in Washington, D.C. There she began writing as an English major. Since new classmates had trouble pronouncing her name, she shortened it to Toni.

Upon graduating, she got a masters degree from Cornell University. Then she took a job teaching English at Texas Southern University in Houston. The black studies program at Southern awakened her interest in black culture. A couple of years later, she returned to Howard University, where she taught for seven years.

In 1965 Morrison went to work as a fiction editor at Random House, a publishing house in New York City. But she longed to write her own novels from an African American perspective. In 1970 her first novel, *The Bluest Eye*, appeared. It recounted the story of a black girl who always wanted blue eyes. Although the book received rave reviews, it was not a commercial success. Morrison's 1973 novel *Sula*, about friendship and community pressures to conform, hit the literary

Acclaimed author TONI MORRISON wrote many popular books in the 1980s. She is perhaps most well known for *Beloved*.

jackpot, winning her national acclaim. *Song of Solomon* followed in 1977 and *Tar Baby* in 1981.

Morrison's first play, *Dreaming Emmett*, about black teenager Emmett Till, who was murdered by white racists in the 1950s, premiered in 1986. The next year, her novel *Beloved* became a best seller and earned her a Pulitzer Prize for Fiction. In 1993 Morrison accepted the Nobel Prize in Literature. Her selection marked the first time a black writer received the honor and the eighth time it was awarded to a woman.

In 1989 Morrison began teaching at Princeton University. She officially retired in 2006, but she continues to teach there. She serves on the editorial board of the *Nation*, a weekly news publication. Her most recent novel is *A Mercy* (2008).

During the 1980s, publishers rediscovered the benefits of publishing series of children's books. Ann Martin's popular Baby-Sitters Club began appearing in 1986. This series, about the adventures of girls who earn money by babysitting, touched a chord with middle graders. Martin cranked out a book a month to meet the demands of her readers before adding other authors to the series. The books proved so profitable that other series, such as Little Sisters and the Baby-Sitter's Club Mysteries, developed from the original.

Individual titles for young people about a variety of topics gained large readerships during the 1980s and became classics. Lois Lowry's *Number the Stars* (1989) told the story of a Danish family determined to save Jews during the Holocaust of World War II. Other favorites included Shel Silverstein's 1981 poetry collection *A Light in the Attic* and Chris Van Allsburg's inspirational Christmas picture book *Polar Express* (1985).

BABY-SITTERS CLUB AUTHOR ANN MARTIN *(center)* signs autographs for fans in 1989. Millions of young girls read the popular novels.

No one covered the range of the written word like Sheldon (Shel) Silverstein. He wrote plays, songs, cartoons, screenplays, and books for readers of all ages. But he's best known for his children's poetry books, especially *Where the Sidewalk Ends* (1974), *The Missing Piece* (1976), *A Light in the Attic* (1981), and *The Missing Piece Meets the Big O* (1981).

The Chicago-born author (1930–1999) began drawing and writing in grade school. It was his way to counter feeling like an outsider. "I couldn't play ball, I couldn't dance. . . . So, I started to draw and to write," Silverstein told a reporter.

While serving in the armed services in the 1950s, he created cartoons for *Stars and Stripes*, a military newspaper. After his service, he illustrated for *Playboy*, a men's magazine. They caught the attention of a New York editor, who suggested Silverstein try creating books for young readers. *Uncle Shelby's Story of Lafcadio, the Lion Who Shot Back* (1963), and *Uncle Shelby's A Giraffe and a Half* (1964) received modest attention. But his 1964 book *The Giving Tree*, a tale about the relationship between a boy and a magical tree, won the admiration of many readers, young and old.

Silverstein's writings showed his quirky personality. He wrote nonsense, stories with many twists and turns, and senti-

SHEL SILVERSTEIN was a multitalented writer in the 1980s. He wrote everything from poetry books for children to screenplays.

mental offerings. His songs contemplated what it would be like to be "A Boy Named Sue" or "The Unicorn." He even attacked yuppies with his play *The Lady or the Tiger Show* (1981), about a television producer who takes unusual risks to improve his show's ratings. Silverstein's nineteen books, thirteen record albums, eight motion picture scores, and at least ten plays have earned him countless awards and a place in the hearts of young readers to this day.

■ NEWSPAPER BEAT

Mergers, buyouts, and a lack of government oversight took a toll on the newspaper industry in the 1980s. In Milwaukee, Wisconsin, the two daily newspapers merged into one. Elsewhere, media companies with television and radio stations gobbled up newspapers as well. They benefited from using the same reporting in different formats, thereby cutting down on staff costs. Another factor hurting the newspaper business was the introduction of all-news radio and cable television in the 1980s. The number of newspapers dropped by about 40 percent from the 1940s high point to 1989.

In 1982 *USA TODAY* hit newsstands, bringing a new look and character to newspapers. *USA TODAY* was the first newspaper to use color, modern graphics, and shorter stories. Unlike most other newspapers, *USA TODAY* aimed at a national audience instead of a local one. Initially, serious newspaper critics made fun of the newspaper for its limited scope and lively presentation. But the format suited many readers who preferred short snippets of news in a modern-looking format.

■ MAGAZINE MANIA

The 1980s saw a rise in the publication of new magazines. In 1980 there were 10,236 magazines. By 1989 the number had climbed to 11,556. Marshall Loeb, the managing editor of *Fortune* (a business magazine founded in 1930), questioned the value of many of the newer magazines, such as *US* and *People*. "[Good] magazines serve the needs of their readers. Today, most magazines just address the wants," he said.

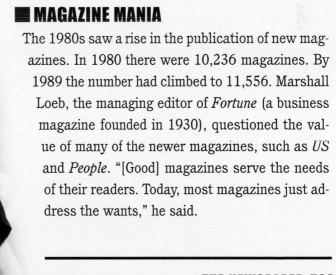

Cathleen Black, publisher of **THE NEWSPAPER *USA TODAY,*** in her office in 1985. The paper launched in 1982.

The average magazine had ninety-eight pages and cost $2.25 an issue. Instead of offering tidbits on a variety of topics, many of the newer magazines focused on specific topics, such as sports, crafts, music, cars, crossword puzzles, celebrities, and computers. Advertisers liked being able to target a particular audience with their messages.

While new magazines appeared on newsstands, many old standbys got makeovers to look bigger and glossier. The magazine with the biggest makeover in the 1980s was *Vanity Fair*, which had not been published in decades. The 1980s version sported glossy celebrity photos on the cover and offered stories with juicy gossip about the lives and scandals of the wealthy. There were also articles on fashion, party-giving, and beauty tips.

Other top-selling magazines also focused on celebrity and status. *People*, begun in 1974, became a magazine powerhouse during the 1980s. Like *Vanity Fair*, its stories often highlighted the lives of the rich and famous. *Us Weekly* covered a similar range of subjects. Founded in 1977 by the New York Times Company, *Us* really took off around 1986. That's when the Times Company sold it to Wenner Me-dia, a group that also produced *Rolling Stone* and *Men's Journal*.

■ NEW WORLD OF COMPUTER MAGAZINES

Magazines on computer technology found a growing audience in the 1980s. The earliest ones, such as *Byte* and *Interface*, educated readers about the infant world of personal computers. These first appeared during the late 1970s and gained a larger readership in the 1980s as more personal computers found their way into people's homes.

The publication of *Personal Computer Age* in 1981 marked the beginning of a new wave of computer-related magazines. This was the first magazine to focus on a specific product. The content was technical and geared to the limited audience that bought IBM Personal Computers, known as IBM PCs. Competitors saw the potential market for this type of magazine. They began publishing their own product-specific magazines, such as those about the Apple II, Atari, and Radio Shack TRS-80 computers. These magazines prospered along with the products they targeted. Once the product became outdated, however, so was the magazine.

■ MAGAZINES FOR YOUNG READERS

During the 1980s, children enjoyed reading magazines such as *Highlights*, which had been around for decades. But new magazines appeared for the younger set too. The Cricket Magazine Group, which had created *Cricket*, added new "literary bugs" for readers of different ages with magazines such as *Ladybug* and *Spider*. The magazines published articles and illustrations by well-known authors and illustrators, including Tomie dePaola, Trina Schart Hyman, Isaac Bashevis Singer, and Eric Carle.

Johnson Publishing, the publisher of *Ebony* magazine, ran *Ebony Jr!* from 1973 until 1985. Similar to the adult *Ebony*, the junior version featured African American history and culture. *Ebony Jr!* targeted black children from five to eleven years of age. Both magazines sought to heighten a sense of community and racial pride among blacks.

The long popular adult magazine *Sports Illustrated* gave birth to *Sports Illustrated for KIDS* in 1989. The weekly magazine immediately caught the interest of athletic middle grade and high school kids. The magazine contained action photos, biographies of athletes, and helpful hints from sports professionals. Many kids who did not usually like to read pored over the magazine's pages, to the delight of their parents and teachers.

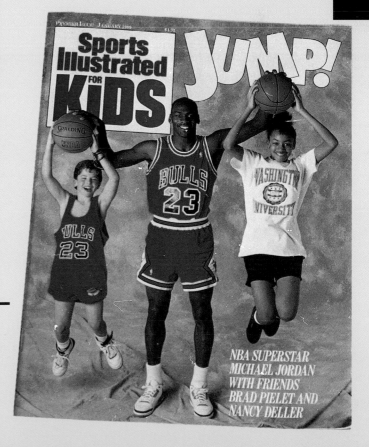

SPORTS ILLUSTRATED FOR KIDS was launched in 1989.

ARTISTS ANDY WARHOL (LEFT) AND JEAN-MICHEL BASQUIAT pose in front of some of their collaborative paintings in 1985. Warhol painted the company logos on their work, while Basquiat added dashes of color and commentary.

CHAPTER SEVEN

FROM GRAFFITI TO PUNK:

VISUAL ARTS, ARCHITECTURE, AND FASHION

Throughout the 1980s, artists experimented with new ways to express their talent, political views, and individuality. Many took their inspiration from already-famous painters, such as Andy Warhol (1928–1987). After achieving fame in the 1960s, Warhol helped along a younger generation of artists, including Jean-Michel Basquiat, David Salle, and Julian Schnabel. In the 1980s, Schnabel fell under the influence of an international art movement called neoexpressionism. Neoexpressionists painted common objects seen on city streets with bold and even violent brushstrokes and unique color combinations. Basquiat and Salle began their careers painting a different type of street art—graffiti.

GRAFFITI ART

Modern graffiti began as an expression of hip-hop culture during the 1970s, usually in the form of spray painted letters and words. Young artists from the inner city never felt comfortable in the formal art world of galleries and museums. So they displayed their talent on building walls, buses, and train cars. Some early graffiti included gang symbols to identify turf. As the designs became more complicated and colorful in the 1980s, graffiti gained attention and status as serious art.

Some communities and the art world embraced graffiti on buildings. Artists received money to create public murals. Art galleries began displaying smaller works of graffiti artists.

Keith Haring began his painting career creating graffiti on public walls. Haring's art featured bold lines and characters and cartoonlike figures. Beginning in the 1980s, he produced a range of wall murals, metal sculptures, and paintings that pleased young and old. When he learned he had AIDS, Haring started a foundation to give money to AIDS research and children's organizations.

ARTIST KEITH HARING originally painted this mural in New York City in 1982, but it was painted over after just a few months. In 2008 the mural was re-created from photographs and unveiled to the public.

The life of the artist Jean-Michel Basquiat reflected the turmoil of youth during the 1980s. He was born in Brooklyn, New York, in 1960. His father was Haitian American and his mother was Puerto Rican. Basquiat showed drawing talent by the age of six. As a teen, he became known as a graffiti artist. By the age of twenty-one, he stopped spray-painting building walls. Instead, he created thick collages that included a startling mix of written political commentary, diagrams, and urban images of cars, buildings, and police.

Once Andy Warhol discovered and promoted Basquiat's talents, his fame soared in the New York art world. His paintings sold at high prices. Basquiat and Warhol painted together and influenced each other's projects. The collaboration boosted Basquiat's star power.

Basquiat became part of Warhol's social scene, which included drugs and a lot of partying. When Warhol died in 1987, Basquiat sank deeper into drugs and became very depressed. He died in 1988 of a drug overdose. But his fame continued. The Brooklyn Museum held a special exhibit of his work in 2005. His paintings continued to sell for ever-higher prices. In 2007 an untitled painting from 1981 sold at auction in New York for $14.6 million.

89

◼ WOMEN ARTISTS

As the women's rights movement of the 1960s and 1970s grew stronger, women artists became bolder. Those who had long done their work in the shadow of men demanded that their art get more notice. They pushed for inclusion in art exhibits, museums, and galleries.

Judy Chicago (born in 1939) found museum doors closed to her after she produced *The Dinner Party* (1979). This breakthrough installation paid tribute to thirty-nine women artists and leaders, from biblical times to modern times. With the help of many artists, Chicago created a dinner table with thirty-nine place settings. Each setting included a variety of arts and crafts, including ceramics, weaving, and painting. Not one to shy away from controversy, she embarked on the even bolder *Birth Project* (1980–1985). Chicago developed and assembled eighty images of birth and creation made by 130 needleworkers worldwide. This time museums were interested. The project toured U.S. museums until 1987. Afterward, individual pieces joined permanent collections in more than thirty institutions and became a permanent installation at the Brooklyn Museum.

Miriam Shapiro expressed her pro-women ideas through a type of collage (a picture made from different materials) she called femmage. She used various materials to form abstract pictures that depicted moments in a woman's life. For example, her 1989 acrylic paint and fabric collage *The Twinning of Adam and Eve in the Garden of Eden* explored the origins of marriage.

New York artist and educator Faith Ringgold (born in 1930), an African American, had battled racism and bias against women artists for decades. In 1980 she created *Ringgold Doll Kits*, the first of several painted dolls. But during the 1980s, she mainly painted her unique story quilts, which focused on black women.

■ CENSORSHIP AND THE ARTS

Throughout the 1980s, tensions increased between conservative members of government and the arts community. Major debates developed about whether taxpayers' money should support art that offended some people's values. The problem was determining whose values must not be offended. A work of art that pleased one group might offend another.

Critics charged that some artists pushed the boundaries of good taste by incorporating religious symbols or nudes in their artwork in a disrespectful way. North Carolina senator Jesse Helms considered this art "obscene or indecent." During the 1980s, Helms frequently used the work of photographer Robert Mapplethorpe as an example of art that should be banned. Mapplethorpe produced a variety of photographs, including portraits of celebrities and still life pictures of objects. During the 1980s, he focused on male nudes, and those photos embraced homosexuality.

Helms railed against the nudes, some believe because Mapplethorpe was a homosexual man with AIDS. One hundred days after Mapplethorpe died of the disease, Helms and his supporters pressured the Corcoran Gallery of Art in Washington, D.C., to cancel a major traveling exhibit of the artist's work.

PHOTOGRAPHER ROBERT MAPPLETHORPE stands in front of one of his photos at an exhibition of his work in New York City in 1985.

The exhibit had been supported by a grant from the National Endowment for the Arts. The public expressed its outrage at the government's censorship, and a private organization stepped in and provided funding for the exhibit.

Other protests erupted to end financial support from the National Endowment for the Arts for controversial work. Opponents felt an installation that included a flag on the floor of the Art Institute of Chicago was unpatriotic. Religious conservatives were appalled after seeing the catalog of visual arts competition winners from the Southeastern Center for Contemporary Art in Winston-Salem, North Carolina. The catalog featured Andres Serrano's "Piss Christ," a photo of Christ on the cross covered in the artist's urine. After revealing such objectionable projects, Helms was able to lead a somewhat successful effort to limit federal funding for the arts.

■ STANDOUT ARCHITECTURE

During the 1980s, some American architects continued to design buildings inspired by the plain, simple structures that had become popular after World War II. Richard Meier and Renzo Piano designed the High Museum of Art in Atlanta, Georgia, with a stark white exterior made of plain paneling. It was awarded the prestigious 1984 American Institute of Architects Honor Award. Deconstructivist architects such as Peter Eisenman, on the other hand, created buildings that looked distorted and unbalanced.

MAYA LIN STANDS IN FRONT OF THE VIETNAM VETERANS MEMORIAL in Washington, D.C., in 1985. Lin designed the memorial when she was a student at Yale University.

AMERICA IN THE 1980s

Artist and architect Maya Lin was born in Athens, Ohio, in 1959. That was ten years after her parents escaped the Communist takeover of China, their homeland. In the United States, her parents taught at Ohio University. Her father created ceramics and became dean of fine arts, while her mother taught literature and wrote poetry. Artistic expression came naturally to their young daughter.

When she was a twenty-one-year-old architecture student at Yale University, Lin designed a Vietnam veterans memorial for a class project. With her professor's approval, she entered it in a contest to see who could come up with the best design for the U.S. Vietnam Veterans Memorial in Washington, D.C. Judges sorted through 1,420 entries and selected her plan.

Lin's simple design showed a wide V-shaped wall of black granite. She envisioned the names of fifty-eight thousand dead soldiers etched into the two connected 247-foot-long (75 meter) walls of stone. Lin sank the booklike walls below ground level. Visitors would read the names of their loved ones from a below-ground-level walkway next to the wall, symbolizing the burial of the dead.

The finished memorial was dedicated in 1982. But Lin's name was never mentioned at the ceremony. After the memorial's construction, an uproar had occurred over its simple and unusual design. To escape her critics, Lin returned to graduate school in architecture. After graduation, Lin designed a Civil Rights Memorial (1989) in Montgomery, Alabama, for the Southern Poverty Law Center, a civil rights education and legal organization. Similar to the Vietnam memorial, this black granite memorial pays tribute to those who lost their life during the civil rights movement.

Over time, critics of the Vietnam memorial changed their minds. More visitors came to pay their respects at this memorial than at any other in the nation's capital. Some laid flowers near a family member's name. Others cried. Lin's former critics came to appreciate how much her memorial honored those who served a nation during a terrible time.

Another school of architects, called postmodernists, wanted to bring back color and decoration. They took their inspiration from much older classical styles. One of the most famous postmodern buildings from the 1980s was Philip Johnson and John Burgee's AT&T Building, completed in 1984 in New York City. The thirty-four-story skyscraper displays sleek, modern lines. But it is crowned with a curving top that resembles fancy furniture from the colonial period. In 1990 the Sony Corporation bought the building and renamed it Sony Plaza.

■ POWER DRESSING

The focus on material possessions and shopping energized the fashion industry in the 1980s. Clothing stores, tanning salons, and beauty shops creating big hairdos prospered. John Molloy's popular book *Dress for Success*, published in 1975 and updated in 1988, guided men on how to look more successful. The author counseled men to wear conservative, expensive clothes and accessories to gain high-powered jobs. Dressing like an executive became known as power dressing. For men the look included dark-colored business suits, light blue or white button-collar dress shirts, and jackets with padded shoulders.

Women of the 1980s followed Molloy's *The Woman's Dress for Success Book* (1977), which displayed a similarly conservative look, with suits, plain silky blouses, and plain, dark high-heeled shoes. The look "was a strong, aggressive silhouette," wrote the British designer John Peacock.

After work, power dressers turned preppy, a look returning from the 1950s. Preppy casual clothes displayed a classic-style similar to business dress. Ironed jeans and khaki pants went with loafers or deck shoes and traditional plaid or striped shirts or turtlenecks. To keep warm, yuppies draped sweaters with crew or V-necks around their shoulders.

Young women model **PREPPY CLOTHING** in 1980 in California. A throwback to the 1950s, the look featured classic clothing such as jeans or khakis and plaid or striped polo shirts.

Yuppy power dresser tastes leaned toward buying brands that screamed "expensive." They preferred clothes designed by Anne Klein, Donna Karan, Ralph Lauren, Gucci, and Calvin Klein, right down to their brand-name underwear. The rising importance of expensive brand-name clothes led designers to display their logos and labels on the outside of clothing and accessories.

A physical fitness craze resulted in specialized clothes to fit every activity. Workout clothes moved out of gyms and dance studios onto the street. Young and old copied clothing from the main female character in the popular movie *Flashdance* (1983). She wore torn jeans or snug-fitting pants covered with leg warmers, and so did eighties athletes and nonathletes alike. Other fashion-conscious Americans wore bodysuits, tights, leggings with stirrups, bicycle and jogging shorts, and tank tops. Designers blended close-fitting fabrics, such as spandex, with cottons and wools for these new sporty outfits.

■ PUNK, GRUNGE, AND IN BETWEEN

Some teens bought into wearing designer clothes. But many more rejected the squeaky-clean expensive look. Jeans remained a mainstay of teen wardrobes. Stores sold jeans acid-washed, stone-washed, ripped, or frayed, either with straight or wide, baggy legs.

Some teens rebelled even more, following fads known as punk, grunge, or rapper styles, which were often inspired by music and film celebrities. Most teens, however, chose fashions somewhere in the middle.

Punk styles originated in Great Britain during the 1970s and had caught on in the United States by the 1980s. Punks covered themselves in black clothing, leather, and piercings. Rings

Actress Jennifer Beals's workout wardrobe from the movie *FLASHDANCE* became a fashion craze after the movie came out in 1983.

In the 1980s, the fashion-style known as **PUNK** had made its way to the United States from Great Britain.

and studs commonly pierced ears, noses, and eyebrows. Some young women also pierced their belly buttons. Fans of the new Music Television (MTV) entertainment and rock videos found inspiration in the singer Madonna's fishnet stockings, chains, and leather.

Both sexes dyed their hair in bright florescent colors. Some men shaved their heads completely. Or they left a line of hair down the middle and added gel to shape spikes in a Mohawk look. Others styled a business cut in front but left hair trailing down the back in a style called a mullet. Some Michael Jackson fans, on the other hand, imitated his black cape, single white glove, and perfectly round Afro hairstyle.

Grunge showed a similar rebellion against materialistic values. Grunge wearers bought clothes that looked old, inexpensive, and used. The baggier the better. Popular rappers wore oversized shirts, backward baseball caps, and wide-legged pants, usually jeans. So did their fans.

Expensive, high-tech athletic shoes completed these outfits. The first Air Jordans and Reebok Freestyles were must-haves, despite their hefty prices, sometimes more than one hundred dollars.

" Though public reaction to Punks was initially one of dismay and fear, as the decade progressed, aspects of the style . . . filtered into both mass-market fashion and high fashion."

—*Valerie Mendes, fashion writer, 1999*

The movie *E.T. THE EXTRA-TERRESTRIAL* debuted in theaters in 1982. Directed by Steven Spielberg, it is one of the highest-grossing movies of all time.

CHAPTER EIGHT

LIGHTS, CAMERA, ACTION:

TV, MOVIES, AND THEATER IN THE 1980s

In the 1980s, movie audiences drove up ticket sales for such blockbuster movies as Steven Spielberg's *E.T.: The Extra-Terrestrial*. Theatergoers enjoyed musical revivals and new European imports, such as Andrew Lloyd Webber's musical *Cats*. And thanks to cable television, TV viewers found channels that catered to a range of tastes, from news to movies.

■ SATELLITES TRANSFORM TELEVISION

Cable television blossomed in the 1980s. The technology had been around for decades. The television signals were delivered through cable lines, instead of over the airwaves, the way traditional broadcast television was delivered. Cable TV was originally developed to help people in remote areas with poor reception. The cable lines gave them access to the same commercial network broadcasts that everyone else was watching.

During the 1960s, cable lines arrived in urban areas and improved TV reception for urban viewers too. The cable systems were small, local services. But three main broadcast networks, ABC, NBC, and CBS, continued to dominate the world of television in the United States.

Things changed in the 1970s and 1980s. Communications satellites improved the technology for delivering cable television. And the U.S. government loosened up its broadcasting regulations. In the late 1970s, cable networks began providing a unique array of programming targeted to specific audiences. Nickelodeon showed children's programs, ESPN specialized in sports, and Showtime offered movies. In 1981 Ted Turner introduced his twenty-four hour news channel, Cable News Network (CNN).

Cable movie channels competed with movie theaters to broadcast the latest films. Meanwhile, other stations captured large segments of the television viewing public looking for unusual programming. Cable networks mushroomed from 3,506 systems (small, locally based networks) with 10 million subscribers in 1975 to 6,600 systems with 40 million customers in 1985. By the late 1980s, cable TV networks had more viewers than the broadcast networks.

Nevertheless, broadcast networks delivered popular evening entertainment in a variety of genres during the 1980s. Long-running urban crime shows, such as *Miami Vice* and *Hill Street Blues*, made stars of their casts. Evening soap operas such as *Dallas*, *Knots Landing*, and *Falcon Crest* appealed to those who liked to see wealthy folks behaving badly. Viewers in their twenties, thirties, and forties enjoyed *thirtysomething*, *Cheers*, and *Moonlighting*, which focused

A popular television drama during the 1980s was **THIRTYSOMETHING**. The cast of the show is shown here in 1988.

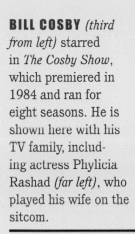

BILL COSBY *(third from left)* starred in *The Cosby Show*, which premiered in 1984 and ran for eight seasons. He is shown here with his TV family, including actress Phylicia Rashad *(far left)*, who played his wife on the sitcom.

on the problems of the Me generation. *Golden Girls*, which premiered in 1985, portrayed the single life for older American women. It was the first show to delve in a respectful and humorous way into the problems experienced by older women.

The most popular family sitcom of the decade was *The Cosby Show*. Comic Bill Cosby broke racial barriers with his all-black television cast. Prior to his show, African Americans appeared mostly as poor, uneducated, or criminal characters. Cosby showed a stable and happy black family with professional parents and normal kids. Other popular family sitcoms took a more satirical approach to family life, including *Family Ties*, *Married . . . with Children*, and *Roseanne*.

Many viewers preferred the growing number of talk shows and news programs to lightweight sitcoms. David Letterman began hosting the talk show *Late Night* in 1982. By the close of the decade, *Oprah Winfrey*, *Arsenio Hall*, *Phil Donahue*, and *Sally Jessy Raphael* had each won a following as a talk-show host. News and current events were the focus of CNN's programs, as well as NBC's *60 Minutes*, ABC's *20/20*, and *Nightline* with Ted Koppel, also on ABC. They, too, attracted large audiences.

❝I hate the word housewife; I don't like the word homemaker either. I want to be called Domestic Goddess.❞

—*comedienne Roseanne Barr, 1982*

OPRAH WINFREY became known nationally in the 1980s, with her successful TV talk show and forays into movies and producing.

Oprah Winfrey rose to television stardom during the 1980s after humble and rocky beginnings. She was born in 1954 in Kosciusko, Mississippi, a poor farm community. Her grandmother raised her until she was six years old. For the next seven years, she lived with her mother in Milwaukee, Wisconsin, where she experienced sexual abuse and poverty. When Winfrey was thirteen, her mother sent her to live with her strict father in Nashville, Tennessee.

Vernon Winfrey worked as a barber. He required his daughter to obey rules, read books, and always do her best. His support turned around the smart but undisciplined girl. While still in high school, Winfrey landed a job at WVOL radio as its youngest broadcaster. After majoring in communications at Tennessee State University, she was offered the coanchor position for WJZ-TV news in Baltimore, Maryland. Then she became a talk show host for Baltimore's *People Are Talking*.

Winfrey's success in Baltimore resulted in an invitation to host WLS-TV's morning talk show *AM Chicago* in 1984. So she moved to the Windy City in Illinois. The show quickly rose to number one among local talk programs. A year later, the station expanded the show to one hour and renamed it *The Oprah Winfrey Show*. Audiences loved Winfrey's smart, warm, commonsense banter. Within another year, the show went nationwide, and eventually it became the highest-rated talk show. In 1988 Winfrey became the youngest person and only the fifth woman to earn the International Radio and Television Society's Broadcaster of the Year Award.

In 1985 Winfrey starred in her first movie, *The Color Purple*, an adaptation of Alice Walker's famous novel, directed by Steven Spielberg. The next year, she appeared in another movie, *Native Son*, and formed her own production company, Harpo Productions. Since then Winfrey has produced several movies for television as well as the 2005 musical *The Color Purple*. In 2000 she added *O, the Oprah Magazine* to her successful media monopoly. *Time* magazine has named her one of the 100 Most Influential People of the Twentieth Century.

In Winfrey's case, money followed fame. *Forbes* magazine counted her on its list of billionaires. Winfrey has used her celebrity for a variety of good causes. She has campaigned against child abuse, built and run a girl's school in South Africa, and started an on-air book club to encourage reading.

Cartoon shows also blossomed during the 1980s. The most popular animated sitcom was *The Simpsons*. It premiered in 1989 and appealed to adults as well as children. This show provided a cynical but funny view of family life and touched on adult topics, such as politics and religion.

To many children of the 1980s, Michelangelo, Donatello, Raphael, and Leonardo were not famous artists. They were names of Teenage Mutant Ninja Turtles. The purple, blue, orange, and red turtles—that walked on their hind legs—first appeared in a 1984 American comic book. They became an instant success and appeared on an animated television show in 1987.

Animated action heroes offered fast-paced entertainment, mainly for school-age viewers. *Dungeons & Dragons*, *G.I. Joe: A Real American Hero*, *Transformers*, *ALF* (for Alien Life Form), and *He-Man and the Masters of the Universe* became after-school and weekend hits. Younger audiences preferred *The Berenstain Bears*, a cartoon version of the popular book series; *Care Bears*; *My Little Pony 'n Friends*; *Pound Puppies*; and *Smurfs*. Increasingly, manufacturers used television characters to sell products, a trend that angered many parents and educators. Stores sold books and toy figures, clothes, and other accessories that featured images and characters from these shows.

TEENAGE MUTANT NINJA TURTLES became very popular in the 1980s. They first appeared in a comic book, which led to a television show and to merchandise, such as the Raphael action figure at right.

■ MOVIES OUT OF THIS WORLD

The eighties was the decade of movie blockbusters. Film studios developed action-oriented spectacles starring actors with box-office appeal. Videocassette recorders (VCRs) gained popularity in the 1980s. Hollywood worried they would keep too many people at home instead of at the movie theaters. But they added to the studios' earnings. Video sales and rentals extended the life of movies, even those with limited audiences in theaters.

Science fiction and fantasy led at the box office. One of the most popular family films of all time appeared in 1982. *E.T.: the Extra-Terrestrial*, by director Steven Spielberg, followed the quest of a young boy to help his friend

Science fiction and fantasy led at the box office.

This **VIDEO RENTAL STORE** is a busy place in 1986. The decade saw a boom in home videocassette recorder sales, with more than half the households in the United States owning a VCR by 1988.

Produced by George Lucas and directed by Steven Spielberg, **RAIDERS OF THE LOST ARK** came out in 1981. It kicked off the profitable Indiana Jones movies starring Harrison Ford.

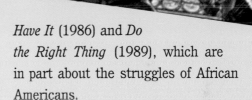

E.T., an alien three million light-years from home, return to his planet. The movie grossed four hundred million dollars, the highest in box office history at the time. Additional fantasy money-makers included Spielberg's action films *Raiders of the Lost Ark* (1981) and *Indiana Jones and the Last Crusade* (1989), director George Lucas's *The Empire Strikes Back* (1980), Ivan Reitman's *Ghostbusters* (1984), and the time-travel *Back to the Future* trilogy (1985, 1989, 1990). *Rambo* (1987), starring Sylvester Stallone, and *The Terminator* (1984), starring Arnold Schwarzenegger, were popular action films.

Brave movies addressed topics not usually covered in films, such as aging and death in *Driving Miss Daisy* (1989), *On Golden Pond* (1981), and *Cocoon* (1985). *Rain Man* (1988) focused attention on autism. Director Spike Lee broke ground with his films *She's Gotta Have It* (1986) and *Do the Right Thing* (1989), which are in part about the struggles of African Americans.

Critics pressured the movie studios to reduce children's exposure to sex and violence in films. In 1984 movie studios bowed to mounting pressure and instituted a PG-13 rating. It indicated that some scenes in a movie may be inappropriate for children under thirteen years of age because of nudity, violence, or swearing. The rating meant theaters could not allow viewers thirteen or under into movies with this designation unless they were with their parents. In reality, the rating did little to change who watched what in American theaters.

DUSTIN HOFFMAN starred in the
motion picture comedy *Tootsie* in 1982.
He received an Oscar nomination for
best actor for the role, in which he
plays a man passing for a woman.

Dustin Hoffman earned a reputation as one of the best character actors in Hollywood. By the 1980s, he had already starred as a down-on-his-luck limping street hustler (*Midnight Cowboy*, 1969), a one-hundred-year-old man (*Little Big Man*, 1970), a foul-mouthed comedian (*Lenny*, 1974), and an overachieving career father (*Kramer vs. Kramer*, 1979). This last role earned him an Oscar.

Born in 1937 in Los Angeles to a jazz musician mother and movie-set decorator father, Hoffman didn't embrace acting at first. But when he was about to flunk out of Santa Monica City College, a friend suggested he take an acting course because "nobody flunks acting." He still left college, but he decided to pursue an acting career. For the next two years, he trained at the Pasadena Playhouse before heading to New York City. In 1961 Hoffman landed his first bit part in a Broadway play in 1961. Other small parts on television and in movies followed. In 1967 he starred in *The Graduate*, a movie about a young college graduate who is seduced by an older woman and falls in love with her daughter. The role was a breakthrough. He established himself as an actor with a wide range of talents.

During the 1980s, Hoffman appeared in two major films that cemented his reputation as a top actor. In the 1982 comedy *Tootsie*, he played an out-of-work actor who disguises himself as a woman to get roles. The movie received ten Academy Award nominations, including Hoffman's fifth nomination as best actor. Although *Ishtar* (1987) proved disappointing, Hoffman received his second Oscar for his role as a man with severe autism in *Rain Man* (1988).

Hoffman has continued to act regularly in films. The college kid who was unsure whether he wanted to act became a star who has appeared in more than forty films and countless television shows. He has won two Academy Awards and six Golden Globes for his work in films and three Emmys for television movies.

■ CATS AND PHANTOMS AT THE THEATER

Two major trends dominated theater in the 1980s. One involved the production of musicals from Europe. British composer and playwright Andrew Lloyd Webber scored a major hit on Broadway with the musical *Cats* (1982). The story turned T. S. Eliot's famous poem *Old Possum's Book of Practical Cats* into a succession of dance numbers performed by actors dressed as felines. The show traveled nationwide and became the longest-running production in Broadway history. Webber followed his four-legged wonders with *The Phantom of the Opera* in 1988. Meanwhile, the French gave U.S. theatergoers *Les Misérables* (1987). This adaptation of Victor Hugo's historical novel mixed opera with serious acting and impressive set design.

The revivals of earlier musical productions became another trend. Updates of *42nd Street* (1980), *My Fair Lady* (1981), and *Brigadoon* (1980) found new audiences. The rock musical *Little Shop of Horrors* (1982) presented a human-eating, talking plant from outer space, which was first seen in the 1960 science fiction movie of the same name. *La Cage aux Folles* (1983), based on a French play, featured the antics of a gay couple dealing with a son's marriage to the daughter of a conservative politician.

Cast members of the musical **CATS** perform at the Tony Awards (given out for excellence in theater in the United States) in 1983. The popular Broadway show debuted in the United States in 1982. The production won seven Tony Awards the next year.

MADONNA performs in concert in 1985. She became immensely popular in the 1980s and by the 2000s was one of the biggest earning musicians in the United States.

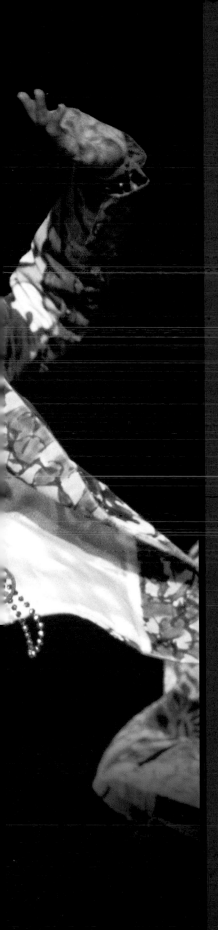

CHAPTER NINE

THE POP MUSIC GENERATION:
MUSIC AND DANCE IN THE 1980s

The famous pop singer Madonna, born Madonna Louise Veronica Ciccone, belted out her approval of 1980s commercialism in her hit song "Material Girl." Through her songs and outrageous dress and actions, this clever businesswoman and singer–shock queen gave everyone permission to be strong, independent spirits. These qualities were reflected in eighties music and dance.

During the 1980s, the music that teens listened to on their Walkmans (a portable cassette tape player) and car radios pained many adults. The folk, Motown, and soft rock of earlier decades had disappeared from most media outlets. Disc jockeys played hard rock, punk, and heavy metal. The louder and angrier the lyrics, the better.

By the late 1980s, the New Kids on the Block provided a change for those who preferred a softer sound. This group of five clean-cut boys from the Boston area, ages twelve to sixteen, sang and danced in an upbeat act. The New Kids on the Block were the first teen group to break into the pop scene. Their sold-out concerts contributed to sales of more than 70 million albums and paved the way for *NSYNC and the Backstreet Boys in the nineties.

■ MTV GENERATION

Music videos were new in the 1980s. These short films, which accompany music by popular bands and singers, are designed as an advertisement for the music. In 1981 the cable network Music Television made its debut. MTV offered a continuous stream of music videos. They were introduced by veejays, or video disc jockeys, who had similar roles to the disc jockeys on the radio. Rock videos played twenty-four hours a day, feeding viewers a diet of rock music and dance along with visuals of spandex, hair bands, and seductive costumes and movements. U2, Bon Jovi, the Cure, Van Halen, Paula Abdul, Janet Jackson, and Duran Duran got their start on MTV. The network also helped longtime rockers, such as Fleetwood Mac, Prince, and Elton John, maintain their popularity. Michael Jackson and Tina Turner revived their careers with music videos on MTV. Jackson performed his classic moonwalk dance moves wearing a trademark right-handed white glove. Madonna cemented her title as queen of pop with sexy moves to thumping beats, accompanied by a chorus line of good-looking men. Adoring audiences copied their favorite musicians' dance moves and dress styles.

MICHAEL JACKSON was just one artist featured on MTV. Fans dressed like him, with one white glove, and copied his dance moves.

MTV played a role in introducing rap artists such as **QUEEN LATIFAH** to a wider audience.

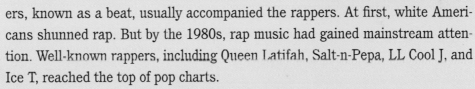

■ HIP-HOP CULTURE

One MTV program, *Yo! MTV Raps,* expanded the audience for rap music. Rap involves saying poems in rhythmic patterns to music with strong beats. Inner city youths developed rap as a way to express injustices they faced in their communities. Instrumental sound tracks from drum machines or electronic synthesizers, known as a beat, usually accompanied the rappers. At first, white Americans shunned rap. But by the 1980s, rap music had gained mainstream attention. Well-known rappers, including Queen Latifah, Salt-n-Pepa, LL Cool J, and Ice T, reached the top of pop charts.

Rap was just one aspect of hip-hop culture. Break dancing was another. It is a form of freestyle street dancing that like rap music became popular in the early 1980s. Break dancing, also called b-boying or b-girling, involves

109

BREAK DANCING was a popular form of dance in the 1980s. This scene is from the hip-hop movie *Beat Street*, released in 1984.

distinct moves that combine gymnastics with dance. In the 1980s, break-dancers competed at parties, at disco clubs, and in the streets to see who could perform the most intricate moves. Sometimes gangs used break dancing competitions as a way to settle arguments.

■ MUSIC FOR A CAUSE

Artists have always used their celebrity to support causes they want to help.

During the 1970s, the world-famous Beatle John Lennon championed peace and environmental issues. In 1980 this work ended with a bullet. A crazed Beatle fan, twenty-five-year-old Mark David Chapman, stalked and shot Lennon as he and his wife, Yoko Ono, were entering their New York apartment building. Lennon's tragic death saddened legions of fans. But Lennon inspired other musicians to continue his quest to improve the world.

FANS OF JOHN LENNON hold a vigil outside Lennon's apartment building, the Dakota, in New York City in December 1980. Lennon was shot outside the building on December 8 by Mark David Chapman.

In 1985 singers Willie Nelson *(left)* and Bob Dylan perform at the first **FARM AID CONCERT**. The concert raised money and awareness for struggling farmers in the United States.

On July 13, 1985, the largest gathering of musicians assembled to produce Live Aid, a live concert to raise money for people starving in Ethiopia, where a drought had created widespread famine. Live Aid used new cable satellite technology to coordinate concerts in Philadelphia and London and to broadcast the program worldwide. The project's success led to other efforts on behalf of those in need. Five months after Live Aid, American musicians held another benefit, this time for U.S. farmers. Country singer Willie Nelson and rockers John Mellencamp and Neil Young organized the star-studded first annual Farm Aid concert in Champaign, Illinois. The concert helped make people aware that U.S. farmers were struggling during tough economic times. Bob Dylan, Billy Joel, Tom Petty, Jon Bon Jovi, and Eddie Van Halen sang at the first event. Elton John, the Grateful Dead, and Garth Brooks joined in later years. By the close of the eighties, Farm Aid concerts raised thirteen million dollars for food and legal help for struggling farm families.

Farm Aid concerts raised thirteen million dollars for food and legal help for struggling farm families.

Left to right: Singers Paul Simon, Kim Carnes, Michael Jackson, and Diana Ross perform the song "WE ARE THE WORLD" as part of USA for Africa in 1985. The proceeds of the song were used to fight hunger in Ethiopia.

1980s

112

AMERICA IN THE

Widespread hunger in Ethiopia took center stage in 1985. For the first time, artists assembled in large numbers to highlight a world disaster. Michael Jackson and Lionel Ritchie wrote the song "We Are the World" after seeing news of starvation and death in Ethiopia. Then the pair invited forty-five pop singers and celebrities to record the song as a group. The group included Tina Turner, Ray Charles, Willie Nelson, Harry Belafonte, Paul Simon, and Bette Midler. They arranged for five thousand radio disc jockeys around the world to play the song. This coordinated effort raised more than forty-four million dollars for poor people in Africa within a year.

Many of the recording artists sang the song at the international Live Aid concert on July 13, 1985. Irish rock stars Bob Geldof and Midge Ure created the concert to raise funds for hunger relief in Ethiopia. They billed their idea as a global jukebox because it reached around the world to alert viewers about the crisis in Ethiopia and the need for donations. A live concert played before 72,000 people in London's Wembley Stadium. Then another concert began in Philadelphia's JFK Stadium, with an audience of 90,000 people. Cable satellite transmitted the concerts to Sydney, Australia, and Moscow, Russia. Live television broadcasts of the concerts reached another 1.5 billion fans in one hundred nations.

Former Beatle Paul McCartney, U2, and Phil Collins led the British performance, while Dick Clark hosted Madonna, Bob Dylan, Elvis Costello, Tina Turner, the Rolling Stones, and more in Philadelphia. Reports after the concert claimed that 95 percent of those who owned television sets watched Live Aid. That was more viewers than watched the 1969 landing on the moon.

■ MUSIC CENSORSHIP

In 1985 Susan Baker, wife of the Republican treasury secretary James Baker, and Tipper Gore, wife of Democratic senator Albert Gore, teamed up. They wanted Congress to pass a law to protect young children from music with lyrics about sex and violence. The two women attended a Senate committee hearing to recommend that record companies place warning stickers on record albums with offensive lyrics. But some saw this as a freedom-of-speech issue. They thought parents should use their own judgment to evaluate what was appropriate for their children.

The rocker Frank Zappa thought teens should be able to listen to his music. He also wondered why parents needed a sticker to tell them the obvious about his albums. His advice: "I would say that a buzz saw blade between the guy's legs on the album cover is a good indication that it's not for little Johnny."

TIPPER GORE *[LEFT]* **TESTIFIES AT A SENATE HEARING** in May 1985 on government regulation of objectionable music lyrics. Susan Baker *(right)* worked with Gore to get record companies to put warning labels on some compact discs and tapes.

> **" Every ballet, whether or not successful artistically . . . has given me something important. "**

—*Mikhail Baryshnikov, Latvian-born ballet dancer, 2008*

■ CLASSICAL MUSIC AND DANCE

Lovers of classical music and ballet may have been outnumbered by rockers in the 1980s. But they still got dressed up and filled concert halls and performing arts centers around the country. In 1980 the Saint Louis Symphony, in Missouri, and the Boston Symphony Orchestra, in Massachusetts, both celebrated their hundredth birthdays.

That same year, the great Russian ballet dancer Mikhail Baryshnikov, became the director of the American Ballet Theatre (ABT), one of the nation's finest ballet companies, based in New York City. New York is one of the dance capitals of the world, with other great companies, such as the New York City Ballet. Like ballet companies everywhere, the New York City Ballet put on annual Christmas productions of the *Nutcracker*, with scores of dancers in twinkling costumes. The company marked its nine-hundredth performance of the ballet in 1981.

The dance world lost two great choreographers in the 1980s. George Balanchine, who had spent about thirty-five years composing dances for the New York City Ballet, died in 1983. Six years later, Alvin Ailey died. Ailey had established his own dance company, the Alvin Ailey American Dance Theater, in 1958. He wanted African American dancers to have a home where they could perform modern dance at a time when they were not welcomed by other companies. (Modern dance encourages dancers to express themselves more as individuals than ballet does.) By the time Ailey died, his New York–based company had become one of the most important modern dance companies anywhere.

In 1982 classical music lovers celebrated the one-hundredth birthday of Igor Stravinsky, a Russian composer. His most famous work is *The Rite of Spring* (1913). As part of the celebration, the great U.S. conductor and composer Leonard Bernstein conducted the National Symphony Orchestra in a performance that was televised around the globe.

Dancer and choreographer Mikhail (Misha) Baryshnikov was born in 1948 in Riga, Latvia, which was part of the Soviet Union at the time. He entered the state ballet school at the age of twelve, a late start for a ballet dancer. At the age of sixteen, he won first prize in the junior division of an international ballet competition. Three years later, he joined the famed Kirov Ballet and had his debut in the ballet *Giselle*. His agile moves and flying leaps made him an instant sensation. Over the next few years, choreographers created ballets to show off Baryshnikov's talents. But he grew restless and felt the Soviet Union limited his opportunities.

In 1974, while on tour in Canada with other Soviet dancers, Baryshnikov decided to remain in the West and asked for asylum. This request to stay meant he could never return home, because he was considered a traitor by the Soviets. While in Canada, Baryshnikov danced with the National Ballet of Canada for a short time. Then he joined the American Ballet Theatre in New York. From 1974 to 1978, Baryshnikov's talents shined in productions of *Don Quixote*, *Cinderella*, and the ever-popular *Nutcracker*, which was filmed for television. For the next two years, he danced with the New York City Ballet and worked with George Balanchine. In 1980 he returned to the ABT as artistic director

MIKHAIL BARYSHNIKOV *(right)* dances with ballerina Susan Jaffe in a performance in Boston in 1988.

and principal dancer.

Baryshnikov acted as well as danced. He appeared in the Oscar-nominated movie *The Turning Point* (1977), *White Nights* (1985), and *Dancers* (1987). By then he had become a U.S. citizen and earned a reputation as one of the world's greatest dancers. Between 1990 and 2002, he served as artistic director of the White Oak Dance Project, which he cofounded with Mark Morris. The touring modern dance troupe featured older, experienced dancers.

To encourage emerging artists of all creative disciplines, Baryshnikov established the Baryshnikov Arts Center in New York in 2005. He continues to dance and tour across the United States and internationally.

AEROBICS CLASSES were one of the hottest exercise crazes
of the 1980s.

CHAPTER TEN

FREE TIME:
SPORTS AND RECREATION

The 1980s offered endless ways to spend free time. In addition to the traditional sorts of games and toys that were available, computer technology added more choices, such as game consoles. But team sports continued to hold their appeal. By the end of the decade, more girls participated than ever before. Many adults who didn't play team sports found other ways to get a physical workout. Exercise was hot!

■ TOYS FOR ADULTS AND KIDS

Several trendy products swept through the nation like a tornado, bringing smiles and filling free time. Canadians Scott Abbott and Chris Haney developed the challenging board game *Trivial Pursuit* for those who liked to test their brains. Hungarian inventor and sculptor Erno Rubik first created the Rubik's Cube in 1974, but it didn't arrive on U.S. shores until 1980. The object of this pattern puzzle was to line up rows of the same colored squares on one side of the cube. Rubik's invention led to books and guides that helped frustrated players find the correct patterns. Since its invention, the handheld riddle has sold more than 10 million units worldwide.

THE CABBAGE PATCH KID was the most popular toy of the 1980s. When the doll first was introduced to the mass market, parents stood in lines at stores to try to purchase them for their children for Christmas presents.

Artistic eighties kids liked drawing with battery-pow- ered Lite-Brites. Younger children played with a rubber doll named Gumby. The 1950s toy was revived by Ed-die Murphy, an actor on the popu-lar late-night TV show *Saturday Night Live*. An animated talk-ing bear named Teddy Ruxpin became another must-have toy. Teddy appealed to kids because he could move his mouth and eyes and tell sto-ries via an audiotape.

The most popular toy, how-ever, was the Cabbage Patch Kid. Cabbage Patch stuffed dolls had no movable parts, and they came with a name, birth certif-icate, and personal story. Art student Xavier Roberts developed the idea for these dolls, which he called Little People. Roberts sculpted and sewed his Little People from pieces of fabric, which he sewed together and stuffed. He sold the Little People at arts and crafts shows for forty dollars, which he called an adoption fee. In 1982 the Coleco toy company bought rights to manufacture the dolls and renamed them Cabbage Patch Kids. They at-tracted a huge national following. By 1990 families had adopted 65 million of them, making them one of the top ten biggest sellers of the decade.

TECHNOLOGY FOR FUN

Pac-Man was one of the first arcade video games offered for personal computers. The round yellow characters with moving mouths arrived from Japan in 1980 and were quickly converted into a game for PCs. The simple game flew off store shelves. Eighteen months after the game's introduction, more than 350,000 games had sold for one billion dollars in the United States alone.

The success of Pac-Man led to other games in a variety of electronic formats. Some games contained holograms—three-dimensional figures produced by a beam of radiation. Games that taught skills, such as *Carmen Sandiego* and *Oregon Trail* for middle graders and teens, and *Reader Rabbit* for preschoolers, became favorites. Other best-selling video games included *Donkey Kong*, *Mario Brothers*, and anything for the Nintendo game console.

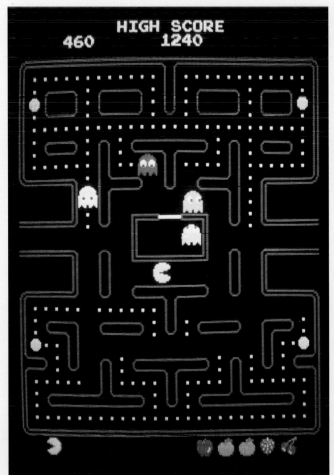

PORTABLE ENTERTAINMENT

Kids played handheld versions of arcade games on their Game Boys, which first appeared in 1989. Game Boys sat in pockets ready to keep bored children happily busy wherever they went. Within three years, customers had purchased 32 million Game Boys.

Adults were more likely to take along a handheld stereo cassette player, one of the hottest new concepts to hit the market.

PAC-MAN led the pack in 1980s video games for computer users to play at home. The game was so popular it inspired an animated television series.

Consumers liked the idea of taking their music with them, and in 1979, Sony introduced the first portable audiocassette recorder, the Walkman. The Walkman's small size and earphones launched a new era of individual music listening. Walkmans went on vigorous walks outdoors and on treadmills at the health club. The popularity of the device threatened sales of traditional LPs, large long-playing vinyl discs with grooves, and stereo record players. By 1983 Walkman outsold LPs by 236 million. The Walkman's great run ended by the mid-1980s, when Sony introduced its portable Discman for playing music on compact discs (CDs).

■ THE AEROBICS CRAZE

By the 1980s, Americans were convinced that regular, vigorous exercise produced the most health benefits. In particular, it helped the heart and circulatory system to work more efficiently. Many doctors believed that for maximum benefit, though, the exercise had to be demanding enough for the exerciser's heart rate to rise above a certain level for at least twenty minutes. Physicians and fitness gurus called this type of exercise aerobics.

Aerobics was still fairly new in the 1980s when actress Jane Fonda gave it her star power. She began producing workout videotapes for people to watch while they exercised at home. Other aerobics enthusiasts put on fashionable

ACTRESS JANE FONDA *(front)* leads an aerobics class in California in 1983. Fonda produced popular workout videos in the 1980s.

In the 1980s, Jane Fonda helped ignite a fitness craze with her exercise videos. (She made eleven of them during the decade.) By then she was famous as an award-winning actress and as a political activist. Born Jane Seymour Fonda in 1937, she is the daughter of actor Henry Fonda. At the age of seventeen, she appeared with her father in the play *The Country Girl*. Four years later, when Fonda was a fashion model, her father introduced her to Lee Strasberg. This noted drama coach saw talent in the young woman. Soon after, she became hooked on acting.

Throughout the 1960s, Fonda averaged two movies a year. She earned praise as a fresh young actress and Golden Globe winner for *A Walk on the Wild Side* (1962). *Cat Ballou* (1965) and *Barbarella* (1968) established her as a serious actress and a sex symbol. During the 1970s, Fonda received two Academy Awards for best actress as a prostitute in *Klute* (1971) and partner of a disabled Vietnam War veteran in *Coming Home* (1978).

By then, Fonda had become an outspoken activist who protested the Vietnam War. In 1972 she visited Hanoi, in the enemy territory of North Vietnam, to campaign against U.S. war policy. She spoke on North Vietnamese radio and posed for photographs that led critics to call her unpatriotic. They gave her the unflattering nickname Hanoi Jane.

Despite the furor, Fonda continued to star in movies into the 1980s. She acted in *On Golden Pond* (1981) with her father. Then she changed direction to take advantage of the fitness craze and promote exercise. Her 1982 book *Jane Fonda's Workout Book* became a best seller. That same year, she produced *Jane Fonda's Workout*, the first exercise video that featured aerobic and strengthening exercises.

Between 1982 and 1995, Fonda completed twenty-three exercise videos, wrote five workout books, and recorded thirteen exercise audiotapes. Since the 1980s, she has written two autobiographies and continued to act in plays and movies. She has also engaged in activities on behalf of women and girls. In 2001 she founded the Jane Fonda Center for Adolescent Reproductive Health at Emory University in Atlanta, Georgia. The main goal of the center is to help adolescent girls avoid pregnancy.

121

spandex outfits and joined aerobics classes at their health clubs. But many Americans preferred to put on a Walkman and go for a jog, a popular form of aerobic exercise. No videos or spandex required!

> **"There's Michael Jordan and then there is the rest of us."**
>
> *—Boston Celtic Larry Bird, 2008*

■ THE PROFESSIONAL SPORTS SCENE

Baseball, football, basketball, and ice hockey attracted large audiences during the 1980s. Televised games increased income for team owners and professional athletes. Baseball drew the largest attendance at games, but football and basketball attracted more television viewers. Almost everyone seemed to watch the Super Bowl. Maybe that's why the Chicago Bears produced a music video, "The Super Bowl Shuffle," in 1986 after they won. The video marked their victory over the New England Patriots, 46–10, the largest margin to that point.

Average salaries for athletes jumped more than 25 percent during the decade. For example, the average baseball player's annual salary rose from $329,408 in 1984 to $597,537 in 1990. Basketball stars could count on salaries into the millions by the end of the 1980s.

Before salaries rose, the National Basketball Association (NBA) had been losing fans during the 1970s. That changed with the 1980 league finals. The games highlighted the

skills of the Los Angeles Lakers players Earvin "Magic" Johnson and Kareem Abdul-Jabbar, and the Boston Celtic newcomer Larry Bird. The Lakers went on to win four other national championships during the eighties. By 1984 a new star appeared, Chicago Bulls draft pick Michael Jordan. Jordan stole the show with his long-shot baskets and heart-stopping jumps. He came from the U.S. Olympic winning team and by the next year was the league's MVP (Most Valuable Player).

One of the top Major League Baseball teams of the decade was the Oakland Athletics. The team led with home-run hitter Mark Mc-Gwire, who hit forty-nine home runs in 1987, his first year in the major leagues. The American League named him Rookie of the Year.

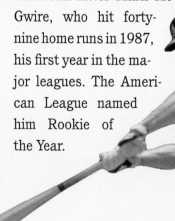

MARK McGWIRE played for the Oakland Athletics baseball team in 1987 and was named Rookie of the Year.

Born in 1963, Michael Jordan needed some patience and persistence when he first began playing basketball. When he was a sophomore at Laney High School in Wilmington, North Carolina, his coach cut him from the team. But Jordan never accepted defeat. He returned to the team two years later. At 6 feet 6 inches (2 m), he was 4 inches (10 cm) taller and determined to do his best.

Jordan earned a basketball scholarship to the University of North Carolina. After his first season, he was named Rookie of the Year. Jordan won the National Collegiate Athletic Association (NCAA) championship for his team by taking a last-minute jump shot, which became his trademark. During his third year at college, in 1984, the Chicago Bulls drafted Jordan. But he waited to start with the team until after he helped the 1984 U.S. Olympic basketball team win the gold.

Jordan thrilled fans with his successful airborne shots and agile leaps. After one season, he was named to the All-Star team and voted the league's Rookie of the Year. In 1988 he was named Defensive Player of the Year, an honor he earned nine times, and MVP for leading in scoring and steals. Once the Bulls added Scottie Pippen, Horace Grant, and John Paxson to the team, the Bulls—and Jordan—became difficult to beat. Between 1991 and 1998, Jordan led the Bulls to six National Basketball As-

CHICAGO BULLS BASKETBALL STAR MICHAEL JORDAN dunks the ball in 1988.

123

sociation (NBA) championships and made the All-NBA Team ten times, earning MVP fourteen times.

Jordan continued the winning streak at the Olympics as part of the 1992 Dream Team, a gathering of unbeatable basketball greats. In 1996 Jordan was named one of the greatest players in NBA history. By then he was a multimillionaire who dabbled in other projects, including acting in the cartoon movie *Space Jam* (1996), endorsing various products on television, launching a cologne line and golf company, and buying and playing with the Washington Wizards. But his crowning achievement remains basketball.

■ OLYMPIC GOLD

The United States hosted the 1984 Olympics in Los Angeles. A record 140 nations participated, though the Soviet Union declined to come. (Soviet leaders were angry because President Jimmy Carter had not sent U.S. athletes to the 1980 Summer Games in Moscow.)

The 1984 Olympics brought several important firsts. For the first time, women ran the same distance as men in marathons. Women's rhythmic gymnastics, cycling road racing, and synchronized swimming became Olympic sports for the first time.

Women attracted considerable attention for outstanding feats. Jackie Joyner-Kersee, one of the greatest all-around U.S. female athletes, earned a silver medal in the 1984 Olympics. In the 1988 Summer Olympics, in Seoul, South Korea, she won gold for the heptathlon. This is a seven-event competition that includes the 100-meter hurdle, high jump, shot put, 200-meter dash, long jump, javelin throw, and 800-meter run. Joyner-Kersee's sister-in-law, Florence (Flo-Jo)

OLYMPIC ATHLETE JACKIE JOYNER-KERSEE gets ready to throw the shot put during the heptathlon competition at the 1988 Olympics in Seoul, South Korea. Joyner-Kersee won the gold in the event.

CARL LEWIS runs in the men's 200-meter dash at the 1984 Olympics in Los Angeles, California. He won four gold medals for the United States that year.

Griffith Joyner, broke world records in the 100- and 200-meter running events at the 1988 Olympic Games. She captured three gold medals at those games. She also captured the world's attention with her grace and speed. (Her many admirers also noticed her long black hair, brightly colored fingernails, and flashy outfits.) Her achievements—though tainted by persistent rumors of steroid use—earned her the title World's Fastest Woman and an appointment as cochair of the President's Council on Physical Fitness and Sports.

Another shining light at the 1984 Olympics was Carl Lewis. He won the gold in the 100- and 200-meter races and again as part of the U.S. 4 x 100-meter relay team. In the 1988 Olympics in Seoul, South Korea, he also won gold for the long jump. He won two more gold medals in the long jump and 100-meter race.

■ AMATEUR TEAM SPORTS

In the 1980s, suburban kids rushed from school to baseball, football, soccer, ice-skating, and cheerleading practice. Urban public schools offered fewer sports, so city kids relied more on park district programs or their own creativity to keep busy and fit. Pickup basketball games allowed players to dream of playing like Michael Jordan or Larry Bird.

Opportunities in team sports improved for women and girls after passage of Title IX. The 1972 law

ordered public schools to give girls the same opportunities as boys to partici-
pate in sports. If schools refused, they would lose financial support from the
U.S. government. For a decade, most high schools and colleges paid little attention to the law, and Supreme Court actions weakened the ruling. To force
schools to comply, Congress passed the 1988 Civil Rights Restoration Act to
restore the intent of Title IX.

By 1989 sports-minded girls were benefiting from both laws. Schools began
offering girls a variety of sports, similar to those offered to boys. And sometimes
they let girls play with the boys. Eighteen-year-old Julie Croteau joined the
NCAA Division III all-male baseball team at Saint Mary's College in Maryland
in 1989. She had played first base that summer for the Fredericksburg (Virgin-
ia) Giants, a semiprofessional team. Croteau played three years on the college
team. Other colleges opened basketball, baseball, and soccer to women.

Schools added **GIRL'S AND WOMEN'S
SOCCER** programs in the 1980s.

During the 1980s, high school coaches organized their first girl's league soccer teams. The National Collegiate Athletic Association, the ruling body for college sports, backed women's soccer tournaments. In 1982 the NCAA hosted its first annual national women's soccer championships. The games inspired high school girls. Within four years, more than 85,000 high school girls were playing team soccer.

In response to growing interest, the National Soccer Hall of Fame and Museum opened in Oneonta, New York, in 1986. Three years later, the National Olympic Committee and U.S. Soccer Federation hosted tryouts for a national team. Women's soccer was not an Olympic sport yet. But women lined up from college and club teams to represent their nation in other world competitions.

■ RECREATION ON WHEELS AND BOARDS

Eighties kids and adults also surfed, roller-skated, snowboarded, and skateboarded. In the early 1980s, Scott and Brennan Olson, brothers and hockey players, designed roller skates with four wheels set in a line. They attached ice hockey boots and rubber toebrakes and began manufacturing their product under the company name Rollerblade, Inc. Since this company made the only in-line skates for years, Rollerblading became the term for all in-line skating.

ROLLER SKATING and later Rollerblading, or in-line skating, provided exercise and a lot of fun in the 1980s.

Former president RONALD REAGAN (LEFT) AND PRESIDENT GEORGE H. W. BUSH pose
together in 1992. The policies of Reagan and Bush defined the 1980s for many Americans.

MOVING PAST THE
"ME! ME! ME!" YEARS

The end of the 1980s stood in marked contrast to the decade's early years, when voters expressed their unhappiness with their lives and the country's direction. In those years, rising oil prices, a sagging economy, and an unfocused foreign policy left the nation feeling glum about the future.

Then along came President Reagan and his sunny speeches. His administration tipped the balance of government "to emphasize family, work and individual responsibility.' Many people at the bottom of the income ladder suffered. Yet Reagan generally made the nation feel good about itself for the first time in decades. Many citizens felt patriotic again, and when Reagan's presidency ended, they looked forward to the next "kinder, gentler" decade that President Bush promised.

■ REAGONOMICS REVISITED

Some Americans, however, resented the Reagan administration's economic policies, which made the rich richer and the poor poorer. Average citizens and small business owners also worried about the number of jobs and small businesses that had been lost. The fault lay partly with an increasingly global economy and the malls and big-box stores sprouting everywhere at home. Reagan's trickle-down theories did not work. The big tax cuts that Reagan gave to the wealthy did not help those at the bottom. Meanwhile, few rules controlled big businesses, which merged at a dizzying pace. President Bush seemed to be following similar policies into the nineties.

Many Americans were uncomfortable with the government's unquestioning support of big business. Many also disliked the importance those with money placed on acquiring material possessions. Others shook their heads over the wild hair, angry rap music, and sexy rock videos of 1980s youth. They saw these trends as a sign the nation was somehow off-kilter and in trouble.

■ ENTERING A NEW ERA

By the close of the 1980s, the United States had become more stable. Under Bush's cautious leadership, the nation responded to a continuation of Reagan's feel-good legacy. With the fall of the Berlin Wall and the breakup of the Soviet Union, the Cold War ended.

The real excitement of the decade involved technology. Eighties inventions changed how people worked, played, communicated, and listened to music. By 1990 desk-sized personal computers allowed users to write and rewrite with the click of a mouse. Accountants created spreadsheets, and anyone with a computer could join a worldwide communications network. Customers began

COMPUTERS ARE LINED UP FOR SHIPMENT at this warehouse in 1991. The computer technology of the 1980s set the stage for radical changes in the American home and workplace.

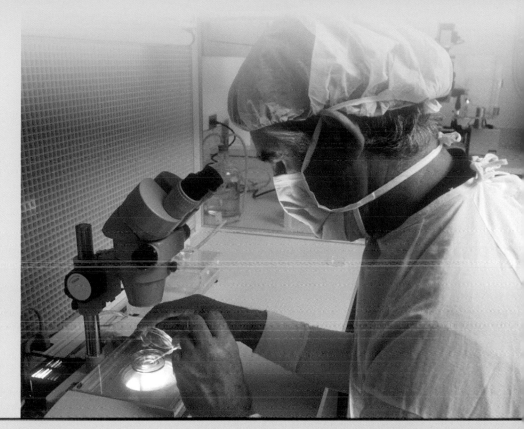

SCIENTIFIC BREAK-THROUGHS SUCH AS IN VITRO FERTILIZATION in the 1980s set the stage for scientific research in the 1990s and 2000s.

using cordless phones and cell phones to communicate. A whole generation embraced technology and the digital age, which began during the 1980s.

In medical and biological sciences, Americans hoped for more milestones. Eighties scientists had already studied human genetics. They explored creating new life from old cells. The challenge for the nineties was to use this knowledge to cure AIDS and other diseases. As the new decade began, Americans waited with enthusiasm for developments in science and technology, and they basked in the new warmth of an international climate of goodwill.

1980
- Eight U.S. servicemen die in a failed attempt to rescue hostages from Iran.
- Inflation increases as prices rise at an average rate of about 13 percent.
- Ronald Reagan is elected the fortieth president of the United States.
- Rubik's Cube, a popular puzzle, arrives in the United States.

1981
- Fifty-two Americans who had been seized in Iran as hostages in 1980 are released after 444 days in captivity.
- President Reagan survives an assassination attempt by John Hinckley Jr.
- Sandra Day O'Connor becomes the first woman on the U.S. Supreme Court.
- The first space shuttle, the *Columbia*, leaves the Florida launchpad on April 12.
- Music Television (MTV) premieres.

1982
- President Reagan signs a bill loosening regulations on the savings and loan bank industry.
- A bomb kills 241 U.S. marines in Lebanon.
- The Equal Rights Amendment for women fails to gain enough support to pass into law.
- Surgeon William DeVries replaces two ventricles in a patient's heart with an aluminum and plastic device.
- *E.T.: The Extra-Terrestrial,* by director Steven Spielberg, is released. It becomes one of the most popular family films of all time.
- Maya Lin's Vietnam memorial is dedicated in Washington, D.C.

1983
- President Reagan proposes the Strategic Defense Initiative (SDI), a space-based defense system, nicknamed Star Wars.
- The United States invades Grenada.
- Congress passes a bill making the third Monday in January Martin Luther King Day.
- Sally Ride becomes the first American woman astronaut in space.

1984
- Reagan wins the election for his second term as president of the United States.
- Scientists identify HIV, the virus that causes AIDS.
- The first baby from a donated egg is born.
- The movie industry adopts the PG-13 rating.
- Apple introduces the Macintosh.
- The United States hosts the Summer Olympic games in Los Angeles.

1985
- Mikhail Gorbachev becomes the leader of the Soviet Union.
- Reagan and Gorbachev hold their first historic meeting in Geneva, Switzerland.
- Live Aid concerts in London and Philadelphia are televised around the world and raise money for Ethiopians suffering from a famine.

1986
- The space shuttle *Challenger* explodes after liftoff, killing all six astronauts on board and the space shuttle program's first passenger, teacher Christa McAuliffe.
- The Reagan administration admits to secretly selling arms to Iran in violation of U.S. law.
- Ann Martin's popular Baby Sitters Club book series begins its publication.
- The Chicago Bears win the Super Bowl over the New England Patriots, 46–10, the largest margin to that point.
- The National Soccer Hall of Fame and Museum opens in Oneonta, New York.

1987
- Ronald Reagan and Mikhail Gorbachev sign the Intermediate-Range Nuclear Forces Treaty (INF), committing the United States and the Soviet Union to reducing nuclear arms.
- On Monday, October 19, the U.S. stock market plunges and stocks lose much of their value. The day becomes known as Black Monday.
- Tom Wolfe's *The Bonfire of the Vanities* exposes the greedy ambitions of a man who works in the world of finance.

1988
- Jesse Jackson Sr. runs for president and registers hundreds of thousands of southern African Americans to vote.
- George H. W. Bush is elected the country's forty-first president.
- For the first time, a commercial e-mail service provider links up with the Internet.
- Compact discs outsell vinyl records for the first time.
- Dustin Hoffman wins an Oscar for his performance in *Rain Man*.
- Andrew Lloyd Webber's British musical *The Phantom of the Opera* opens on Broadway, becoming a smash hit.

1989
- The Berlin Wall comes down in Germany, signaling the breakup of the Soviet Union and the end of the Cold War.
- President Bush orders the invasion of Panama and removes Manuel Noriega from power there.
- The Federal Deposit Insurance Corporation (FDIC), which had been covering the losses of savings and loan banks, runs out of money.
- The United States' national debt ($2.6 trillion) is triple what it was in 1980.

8   Mike Wallace, *Between You and Me* (New York: Hyperion, 2005), 46.

8   Ibid., 48.

10 Ronald Reagan, "Time to Recapture Our Destiny," speech, Detroit, July 17, 1980, *Ronald Reagan Presidential Foundation and Library*, n.d., http://www.reaganfoundation.org/reagan/speeches (October 11, 2006).

11 Harold Evans, *The American Century* (New York: Alfred Knopf, 2000), 612.

12 Peter Jennings and Todd Brewster, *The Century* (New York: Doubleday, 1998), 463.

13 Ronald Reagan, "First Inaugural," *Ronald Reagan Presidential Foundation and Library*, n.d., http//www.reaganfoundation.org/reagan/speeches (October 20, 2006).

15 Chris Matthews, *American: Beyond Our Grandest Notions* (New York: Free Press, 2003), 186.

15 Ronald Reagan, *Ronald Reagan: An American Life* (New York: Simon & Schuster, 1990), 261.

16 Ibid., 13–14.

19 George Tindall and David Shi, *America: A Narrative History*, 6th ed., vol. 2 (New York: W. W. Norton & Company, 2004), 1,182.

21 Arthur Schlesinger Jr., *The Almanac of American History* (New York: Barnes & Noble, 1993), 616.

21 Paul Slansky, *The Clothes Have No Emperor: A Chronicle of the American '80s* (New York: Simon & Schuster, 1989), 116.

22 Cannon, 196.

22 Gil Troy, *Morning in America: How Ronald Reagan Invented the 1980s* (Princeton, NJ: Princeton University Press, 2005), 209.

23 Lorraine Glennon, ed., *Ladies Home Journal 100 Most Important Women of the 20th Century* (Des Moines: Meredith Corporation, 1998), 35.

26–27 Kenneth Walsh, "What History Has to Say," *U. S. News and World Report*, May 29, 2006, 46.

27 Kenneth Davis, *Don't Know Much about History* (New York: Avon Books, 1990), 417.

28 Bill Moyers, *A World of Ideas: Conversations with Thoughtful Men and Women about American Life Today and the Ideas Shaping Our Future*, ed. Betty Sue Flowers, (New York: Doubleday, 1989), 275.

28 Jennings and Brewster, 507.

29 Reagan, *An American Life*, 13.

30 Evans, 647.

30 Richard Reeves, "My Years with Ronald Reagan: What a Skeptical Biographer Discovered about a Very Elusive Subject," *American Heritage*, February–March 2006, 50.

30 Wallace, 61.

31 *Ebony*, "Ebony Interview with the Rev. Jesse Jackson," June 1981, 155.

32 John Ehrman, *The Eighties: America in the Age of Reagan* (New Haven, CT: Yale University Press, 2005), 164.

33 Dean Lacy, "Electoral Support for Tax Cuts: A Case Study of the 1980 American Presidential Election," *American Politics Quarterly*, July 1998, 288.

33 White House, "Biography of George H. W. Bush," *White House*, n.d., http://www.whitehouse.gov/history/presidents/gb41 (September 9, 2006).

34 Reagan, *An American Life*, 683.

34 Jennings and Brewster, 520.

40 Evans, 626.

41 Ibid.

42 Jennings and Brewster, 478.

43 Tindall and Shi, 1,188.

43 Jennings and Brewster, 484.

43 Ibid.

46 Troy, 225.

47 Moyers, 60–61.

47–48 Evans, 642.

48 Timothy Curry and Lynn Shibut, "The

Cost of the Savings and Loan Crisis: Truth and Consequences, *FDIC Banking Review*, 33 (October 11, 2006).

48 Tindall and Shi, 1,194.

60 Ronald Reagan, "Challenger," *Ronald Reagan Presidential Foundation and Library*, n.d., http://www.reaganfoundation.org/reagan/speeches/speech.asp?spid=23 (October 11, 2006).

60 Jennings and Brewster, 494.

62 Sasha Alyson, *You Can Do Something about AIDS* (Boston: Stop AIDS Project, 1990), 28.

63 Marlene Targ Brill, *Extraordinary Young People*, (Danbury, CT: Children's Press, 1992), 157.

65 Tindall and Shi, 1,194.

66 Barbara Ehrenreich, *Fear of Falling: The Inner Life of the Middle Class* (New York: Pantheon, 1989), available online at *Northern Illinois University*, n.d., http://www3.niu.edu/~td0raf1/labor/Ehrenreich%20on%20Yuppies (November 10, 2006).

67 Susan Faludi, *Backlash: The Undeclared War Against American Women* (New York: Doubleday, 1991), 1.

68 Roberta Francis, "The History Behind the Equal Rights Amendment," *National Council of Women's Organizations*, n.d., http://www.equalrightsamendment.org/era (October 27, 2006).

68 Kiron Skinner, ed., *Reagan: A Life in Letters* (New York: Free Press), 249.

73 Moyers, 141.

75 Michael Tubridy, "Defining Trends in Shopping Center History," *Research Review*, 2006, 13.

75 Ehrenreich.

75 Tom Wolfe, "The Me Decade and the Third Great Awakening," *New York*, August 23, 1978, 18.

82 *Publisher's Weekly*, "Shel Silverstein Biography," February 24, 1975, n.d., http://www.geocities.com/SunsetStrip/Club/6166/ss/ssbiohtml (November 3, 2006).

83 Samir Husni,"Are There Too Many Magazines?" *Folio: The Magazine*, 91, in *Magazine Management*, November 1, 1991.

90 Schlesinger, 631.

93 John Peacock, *The 1980s: Fashion Source-books* (New York: Thames and Hudson, 1998), 7.

95 Valerie Mendes, *20th Century Fashion* (New York: Thames & Hudson, 1999), 222.

99 QuotationsPage.com and Michael Moncur, "Roseanne Barr Quotes," *The Quotations Page*, n.d., http://www.quotationspage.com/quotes/Roseanne_Barr (November 20, 2006).

104 IMDB.com, "Dustin Hoffman— Biography," *Internet Movie Database*, n.d., http://www.imbd.com.nana/nm0000163/bio (November 20, 2006).

113 Slansky, 141.

114 Kennedy Center, "Biographical Information for Mikhail Baryshnikov," *Kennedy Center*, n.d., http//www.kenney-center.org (December 12, 2008).

122 NBA, "Michael Jordan Bio.," *National Basketball Association*, n.d., http://www.nba.com/history/players/jordan_bio.1 (December 22, 2008).

129 David Brooks, "The Era of What's Next," *New York Times*, October 26, 2006, A27.

129 Troy, 327.

SELECTED BIBLIOGRAPHY

Below is a sampling of the books the author used for her research. She also consulted articles from the *New York Times*, the *Chicago Tribune*, the *Chicago Sun-Times*, the *Nation*, the *Historian*, *Oregon Business*, *Presidential Studies Quarterly*, and online sources.

Caplow, Theodore. *The First Measured Century*. Washington, DC: AEI Press, 2001.
This title offers statistics, graphs, and analysis of U.S. trends about everything from the economy to government to social issues.

Evans, Harold. *The American Century*. New York: Alfred Knopf, 2000.
This overview of the twentieth century covers social and political movements and the people who led them.

Felder, Deborah. *A Century of Women: The Most Influential Events in Twentieth-Century Women's History*. Secaucus, NJ: Carol Publishing, 1999.
The author focuses on how women have influenced key events in U.S history.

Jennings, Peter, and Todd Brewster. *The Century*. New York: Bantam, Doubleday, 1998.
This title, by a top news reporter, provides one of the most comprehensive overviews of the twentieth century.

LaFerber, Walter. *America, Russia, and the Cold War: 1945–1984*. New York: Knopf, 1985.
This historian explores U.S.-Soviet relations since 1945 in the context of Cold War relations.

Moyers, Bill. *A World of Ideas: Conversations with Thoughtful Men and Women about American Life Today and the Ideas Shaping Our Future*. Edited by Betty Sue Flowers. New York: Doubleday, 1989.
In 1988 television newscaster Bill Moyers interviewed men and women from many disciplines for the PBS series *A World of Ideas*. This book reproduces those interviews with authors, educators, politicians, scientists, and historians.

Payne, Barbara, ed. *Eyewitness to the 20th Century*. Washington, DC: National Geographic Society, 1998.
Trends, trivia, and photographs highlight this trip through the twentieth century.

Reagan, Ronald. *The Reagan Diaries*. Edited by Douglas Brinkley. New York: HarperCollins, 2007.
The editor examines entries from Reagan's diaries to get an inside look at what motivated and touched the president.

————. *Ronald Reagan: An American Life*. New York: Simon & Schuster, 1990.
This autobiography provides some insights into how Reagan evolved from actor to president.

Riley, Glenda. *Inventing the America Woman*. Arlington Heights, IL: Harlan Davidson, 1986.
The book delves into the history of women in the United States.

Schlesinger, Arthur M., Jr., ed. *The Almanac of American History*. New York: Barnes & Noble, 1993.
The author looks at key events and people during the twentieth century, using the format of an almanac.

Smith, Lissa, ed., *Nike Is a Goddess: The History of Women in Sports*. New York: Atlantic Monthly Press, 1998.
This overview of women in sports covers important women athletes and women's sports events throughout the last century.

Targ, Harry. *Strategy of an Empire in Decline: Cold War II*. Minneapolis: MEP Publications, 1986.
This title examines U.S. foreign policy since World War II, focusing on the Carter and Reagan administrations.

Troy, Gil. *Morning in America: How Ronald Reagan Invented the 1980s*. Princeton, NJ: Princeton University Press, 2005.
This title provides a critical look at the influence image-oriented president Ronald Reagan had on the United States and on the American presidency.

TO LEARN MORE

Books

Allen, Amy Ruth. *Queen Latifah*. Minneapolis: Twenty-First Century Books, 2001.
This biography tells the story of one of the first successful female hip-hop artists.

Batchelor, Bob. *The 1980s*. American Popular Culture through History series. Westport, CT: Greenwood Press, 2006.
This overview of the decade analyzes pop culture and how it relates to historic events.

Baudot, Francois. *Elle Style: The 1980s*. New York: Filipacchi, 2003.
The book describes 1980s fashions and popular fads, and it also touches on cultural events.

Benson, Michael. *Ronald Reagan*. Minneapolis: Twenty-First Century Books, 2004.
This biography chronicles the rise of Ronald Reagan from actor to governor to president.

Brill, Marlene Targ. *Extraordinary Young People*. Danbury, CT: Children's Press, 1996.
This collection of biographies highlights the lives of boys and girls who accomplished important things during their early years. Many were children and teens during the 1980s, including Tiger Woods and Ryan White.

Childress, Diana. *George H. W. Bush*. Minneapolis: Twenty-First Century Books, 2007.
This book describes the life and presidency of the first President Bush.

Gherman, Beverly. *Jimmy Carter*. Minneapolis: Twenty-First Century Books, 2004.
This young adult biography recounts the life of the thirty-ninth U.S. president.

Gourley, Catherine. *Ms. and the Material Girls: Perceptions of Women from the 1970s through the 1990s*. Minneapolis: Twenty-First Century Books, 2008.
This title in the Images and Issues series discusses the social and political representations of American women during the 1970s through the 1990s.

Jennings, Peter. *The Century for Young People*. New York: Doubleday, 1999. This rich overview of the twentieth century was written by one of the top news reporters and anchors. The lively text is supplemented with plenty of action photos.

Kallen, Stuart. *The 1980s: A Cultural History of the United States through the Decades*. San Diego: Lucent Books, 1999.
The author reviews the origins of rap music and explores how rappers have influenced language, dance, and fashion.

Krohn, Katherine. *Oprah Winfrey: Global Media Leader*. Minneapolis: Twenty-First Century Books, 2009.
Learn about Oprah's rise to global television dominance in this biography.

Lesinski, Jeanne M. *Bill Gates: Entrepreneur and Philanthropist*. Minneapolis: Twenty-First Century Books, 2009.
This biography details Bill Gates incredible success with computer software company Microsoft.

Websites

"African-Americans in the Twentieth Century."
http://www.liu.edu/cwis/cwp/library/african/2000/century.htm
This site offers a decade-by-decade review of African American history and culture during the twentieth century. The overview of the 1980s, for example, notes the nomination of Henry (Hank) Aaron to the Baseball Hall of Fame and the celebration of Martin Luther King Jr.'s birthday as a federal holiday.

American Cultural History: 1980–1989
http://kclibrary.lonestar.edu/decade80.html
This site gives a snapshot of each decade in the twentieth century, including the 1980s. It surveys many of the same topics included in this book. Everything from binge buying and politics to movies, fashion, and architecture are covered.

America's Story from America's Library
http://www.americaslibrary.gov
The Library of Congress continues to add biographies of famous Americans, original documents, and overviews of important eras in U.S. history.

Film History of the 1980s
http://www.filmsite.org/80sintro.html
The site features movie trends and highlights the best films, actors, and directors of the 1980s.

George Bush Presidential Library and Museum
http://bushlibrary.tamu.edu
The site provides archival material related to the first Bush presidency, including photos and biographical information. Visitors can download an audio tour of the museum.

Ronald Reagan Presidential Foundation and Library
http://www.reaganfoundation.org
The site displays colorful photos of exhibits at the library, such as a presidential motorcade and the inside of Air Force One. It also contains a documents archive related to Reagan's presidency.

Films

The 20th Century: The 1980s: A Decade of Decadence. VHS. Orland Park, IL: MPI Home Video, 2000.
This review of the decade focuses on Ronald Reagan and on right-wing politics. It also portrays the new MTV generation.

Video Rock Attack. VHS. London: PolyGram Filmed Entertainment, 2000.
The video features a collection of different rock artists from the 1980s, such as Dire Straits, Soft Cell, and Dexys Midnight Runners.

SELECTED 1980s CLASSICS

Books

Turow, Scott. *Presumed Innocent*. New York: Farrar, Strauss & Giroux, 1987.
The story follows a legal prosecutor charged with the murder of his colleague. This book was one of the first of many detective legal thrillers.

Walker, Alice. *The Color Purple*. New York: Harcourt Brace Jovanovich, 1982.
This Pulitzer Prize-winning novel by Alice Walker is about an abused and uneducated black woman's struggle for empowerment. The book was praised for the depth of its female characters and for its use of black English vernacular.

Wolfe, Tom. *The Bonfire of the Vanities*. New York: Farrar, Strauss & Giroux, 1987.
In this novel about greed, racism, and ambition, Wolfe gives the reader a vivid taste of what life was like in New York during the 1980s—for people like the fabulously wealthy and arrogant bond trader, Sherman McCoy, but also for people who were far less fortunate.

Films

Chariots of Fire. 1981. DVD. Burbank, CA: Warner Home Video, 2007.
Ben Cross and Ian Charleson portray two real-life British track athletes, one Jewish and one a
devout Scottish missionary, who compete in the 1924 Olympics.

Silkwood. 1983. DVD. Los Angeles: MGM, 2003.
In this true story, Meryl Streep plays the factory worker Karen Silkwood. Silkwood was murdered
while trying to expose serious safety violations at the plutonium plant where she worked.

When Harry Met Sally. 1989. DVD. Los Angeles: MGM, 2001.
In this romantic comedy, Billy Crystal and Meg Ryan play two friends who wonder whether men
and women can ever be just friends.

1980s ACTIVITY

Identify six to ten things in your own life or family or community history
that relate to the 1980s. (To start your thinking, consider your parents',
grandparents' or neighbors' lives; family antiques or collections; your house or
buildings in your neighborhood; favorite movies, books, songs, or TV shows; or
places you've visited.) Use photographs, mementos, and words to create a print
or computer scrapbook of your 1980s connections.

141

143

ABOUT THE AUTHOR

Marlene Targ Brill is an award-winning author of nearly seventy books for readers of all ages. Her passion is writing about key events in history and the people who made them possible. She has written five titles in this series and wrote several other titles about important people in history, including *Michelle Obama: From Chicago's South Side to the White House* and *Marshall 'Major' Taylor: World Champion Bicyclist*.

PHOTO ACKNOWLEDGMENTS

The images in this book are used with the permission of: © Jon Gray/Stone/Getty Images, p. 3; AP Photo/File, pp. 4–5; © Michael Grecco/Getty Images, pp. 7, 140 (right); © Bettmann/CORBIS, pp. 8, 9, 24–25, 35, 105; AP Photo, pp. 10–11, 21, 37, 43, 53, 76–77, 85, 111, 119, 122; Courtesy Ronald Reagan Library, pp. 12, 14, 15, 18, 26, 29, 71, 140 (left); © Arthur Grace/ZUMA Press, p. 13; © Lee Frey/Authenticated News/Getty Images, p. 17; © Cindy Karp/Time & Life Pictures/Getty Images, p. 19; © Peter Jordan/Time & Life Pictures/Getty Images, p. 20; © Diana Walker/Time & Life Pictures/Getty Images, pp. 22, 128–129; Library of Congress (LC-USZ62-86846), p. 23; © Terry Ashe/Time & Life Images/Getty Images, p. 27; © Bill Pierce/Time & Life Pictures/Getty Images, p. 31; © David Valdez/Time & Life Pictures/Getty Images, p. 32; AP Photo/Peter Southwick, p. 33; REUTERS/David Brauchli JDP, p. 34; © Wally McNamee/CORBIS, pp. 38, 113; AP Photo/Charles Knoblock, p. 40; © Adam Bartos/Time & Life Pictures/Getty Images, p. 45; © Jim West/ZUMA Press, p. 46; AP Photo/John Duricka, p. 48; AP Photo/Peter Morgan, p. 49; AP Photo/Sal Veder, pp. 50–51; © Doug Wilson/CORBIS, p. 52; AP Photo/Paul Sakuma, p. 54; © Ben Martin/Time & Life Pictures/Getty Images, p. 55; © Shelly Katz/Time & Life Pictures/Getty Images, p. 57; NASA/JSC, p. 59; NASA/KSC, p. 60; AP Photo/Mark Lennihan, p. 62; © ZUMA Press, p. 63; © Ernst Haas/Premium Archive/Getty Images, pp. 64–65; © James Fiedler Jr./Washington Times/ZUMA Press, p. 67; © Cynthia Johnson/Time & Life Pictures/Getty Images, pp. 68, 83; Lambert/Hulton Archive/Getty Images, p. 69; © T. Lanza/National Geographics/Getty Images, p. 72; AP Photo/William Smith, p. 74; © Bachrach/Hulton Archive/Getty Images, p. 78; © Harcourt Brace/Hulton Archive/Getty Images, p. 79; © Ted Thai/Time & Life Pictures/Getty Images, pp. 80, 102–103; © Marianne Barcellona/Time & Life Pictures/Getty Images, p. 81; © Sony BMG Music Entertainment/Getty Images, p. 82; AP Photo/Richard Drew, pp. 86–87; © Matthew Roberts/ZUMA Press, p. 88; © Rose Hartman/CORBIS, p. 91; © James P. Blair/National Geographic/Getty Images, p. 92; © George Rose/Getty Images, p. 93; © Paramount/courtesy Everett Collection, pp. 94, 103; © Dave Hogan/Hulton Archive/Getty Images, p. 95; © Universal/courtesy Everett Collection, p. 96; © MGM Television/ courtesy Everett Collection, p. 98; AP Photo/G. Paul Burnett, p. 99; © King World Productions/courtesy Everett Collection, p. 100; AP Photo/Julia Malakie, p. 101; © Columbia Pictures/courtesy Everett Collection, p. 104; © Neal Preston/CORBIS, pp. 106–107; © Tony Bock/Toronto Star/ZUMA Press, p. 108; © Janette Beckman/Redferns/Getty Images, p. 109 (top); Everett Collection, pp. 109 (bottom), 112; © Hulton Archive/Getty Images, p. 110; AP Photo/Elise Amendola, p. 115; © Jon Gray/Stone/Getty Images, pp. 116–117; © Jacques Chenet/Time & Life Pictures/Getty Images, pp. 118, 140 (middle); AP Photo/Reed Saxon, p. 120; AP Photo/John Swart, p. 123; AP Photo/Lennox McLendon, p. 124; AP Photo/Lionel Cironneau, p. 125; © Duomo/CORBIS, p. 126; © SuperStock, Inc./SuperStock, p. 127; © Douglas Burrows/Liaison/Getty Images, p. 130.

Cover: © Bernard Gotfryd/Premium Archive/Getty Images (top left); © Richard E. Aaron/Redferns/Getty Images (top right); © Ralph Morse/Time & Life Pictures/Getty Images (bottom left); Courtesy Ronald Reagan Library (bottom right).